City and Islington Sixth Form College
Library
The Angel 283-309 Goswell Road
London EC1V 7LA

T: 020 7520 0652
E: sfclib@candi.ac.uk

CITY AND ISLINGTON
COLLEGE

This item is due for return on or before the date last stamped below.
You may renew by telephone, email or online. Please quote your
student ID if renewing by phone.

Fine: 5p per day

CPD6017

Contents

What view of the world does *Emma*
leave us with?   106

NOTES

Introduction

"A heroine whom no-one but myself will much like," the author famously proclaimed. In fact, in any league of likeability Miss Woodhouse is streets ahead of Miss Fanny – the ostentatiously "meek" heroine of *Mansfield Park*. Meek Emma is not. Indeed it is her sense of absolute sovereignty over her little world of Highbury – her right, as she presumes, to dispose of the marriage choices of those in her circle – which brings her to grief. And that grief, by the familiar course of the heroine's moral education in Austen's fiction, makes her, through remorse and repentance, a mature woman capable of forming correct judgements. Not least about whom Miss Woodhouse herself will marry.

Some of Austen's heroines are encountered in conditions of hardship (Fanny Price again), or facing a lonely future (Anne Elliot), or in relative penury (Catherine Morland). None of these apply to Emma. As the novel opens we are informed that she is "handsome, clever, and rich". The happiest of Austen's heroines at the outset, she comes close to being the unhappiest when her match-making schemes go all awry and her protégée, Harriet Smith, becomes her Frankenstein's monster.

Emma, of all the six great novels, is the one which conforms most closely to Austen's famous formula (expressed to a friend as she was writing *Emma*) that "three or four families in a country village is the very thing to work on", or the sarcasm she directed against herself about the "little bit (two inches wide) of ivory on which I work".

Emma is, by general agreement, the "quietest" of the novels. The critic Maria Edgeworth's private complaint that "there is no story in it" is cited by those who find it culpably lacking in incident, or excitement. Others, however, find the plot in *Emma* the most successful Austen achieved. It is, for example, unusual among the sextet in playing a cunning trick on the reader who – unless they are sharp (sharper certainly than Miss Woodhouse) – may well be deluded as to which eligible young (or less than young) man the heroine will end up spending the rest of her life with. Or whether, given her frequently uttered distaste for marriage, she will end up the only unwed of the six heroines at the end of it all.

A summary of the plot

Emma has a deceptively simple plot which is easy enough to summarise, but teasingly complex as one reads it on the page. It is the only one of Austen's novels which has, as its title, the heroine's name – predicting the close focus which the narrative will have on Miss Emma Woodhouse and her fortunes.

She is rich, clever, and nearly 21 – three facts which alert the reader that, coming into adulthood and her fortune, as she is, Emma will be a prize on the marriage market. Emma's elder sister, Isabella ('Belle' – considerably less clever) has married a local man, John Knightley, who is now a rising barrister in London. They have four children. A fifth is born during the course of the narrative. Emma's mother, after whom she is said to "take", died some years since. Emma devotes herself to the care of her valetudinarian and semi-invalid father. The Woodhouses have for generations been the leading family in Highbury – whose confines the narrative never leaves (something else which makes this novel different from Austen's other five, where different settings are prominent features).

As the action opens Emma has triumphantly disposed of her governess, Miss Taylor, to a middle-aged local neighbour, Mr Weston. He is prosperous, but of a slightly lower class than the Woodhouses. Such small social differences are of great significance in Highbury – a fictional location based on the small agricultural towns which Austen knew from her own county, Hampshire. Enthused by what she thinks is her success in match-making, Emma rashly befriends Harriet Smith, a senior pupil at the local school. Harriet is illegitimate – the daughter of who knows (a tradesman, it later emerges, who lives well away from Highbury). Emma persuades Harriet to give up her plans to marry an eminently suitable young farmer, Robert

Martin, scheming instead to marry Harriet to the recently arrived young clergyman, Mr Elton. Mr Elton appears to play along but his interest is actually in Emma, not Harriet. Emma ignores the warnings of her oldest friend, Mr Knightley, the 37-year-old local squire and older brother of John Knightley, who perceives what is really going on. On the way back from a Christmas party at the newly-married Westons' house, all becomes clear to Emma when a tipsy Mr Elton finally plucks up the courage to propose to her. She is disgusted by his absurd pretensions. Her matchmaking plans, humiliatingly, have come to nothing.

Highbury is put into a flutter by the imminent arrival of two new faces. Mr Weston's son, Frank, by his first marriage – now adopted by wealthy in-laws and renamed by them "Churchill" – is coming to the town for the first time. (He did not, oddly, attend his father's wedding.) He is a dashing, eligible bachelor of a kind rare in Highbury. Another new arrival is Jane Fairfax, who has come to stay with her relations, the elderly Mrs Bates and the middle-aged Miss Bates, a genteel couple left in penury by the death of the Revd Bates, an earlier occupant of the vicarage. Jane is a governess, and highly cultivated. An orphan, her ostensible reason for coming to Highbury is a worrying cold, but there may be another reason – as Mr Knightley, the keenest observer in the community, suspects. The paths of

Jane and Frank have, we learn, crossed at the seaside town, Weymouth, where she was the companion-tutor of a young lady. Emma has an instinctive dislike for the accomplished Miss Fairfax, and barely manages to disguise it. But she is fascinated by Frank Churchill and fancies that he may be falling in love with her.

She is flattered by his attentions but thinks he might be a suitable match for Harriet, about whom she feels guilty. Frank mischievously encourages Emma to think that there is some illicit sexual reason for Jane Fairfax's having left the family with whom she was employed. He is, it later emerges, throwing dust in her face. The truth is very different.

Mr Elton returns from the marriage market at Bath with a rich wife, the former Miss Augusta Hawkins. Mrs Elton proves as vulgar and as imperious as her Christian name predicts. Mr Elton continues to be brutally rude to Harriet, fuelling Emma's dislike of the vicar and his wife. Things come to a head on a picnic organised by Mrs Elton where Emma loses control of herself, flirts with Frank Churchill and is unforgivably rude to the stupid and garrulous Miss Bates, for which Mr Knightley rebukes her. She is bitterly ashamed. Her cup of bitterness continues to overflow as she suspects that Harriet may be Mr Knightley's intended. Everything resolves itself when it emerges, to everyone except Mr

Knightley's surprise, that Frank is secretly engaged to Jane. By this point, Emma has realised that she is in love with – has long been in love with – Mr Knightley. The novel, which began with a marriage, ends with a trio of them: Harriet to her farmer, Jane to Frank, and Emma to Mr Knightley. The newly married Revd Elton presides.

What is *Emma* about?

Emma is set in a small, claustrophobic provincial world – a world from which, for the heroine and most of the characters, there is no escape. It is not a world which has entranced everyone. Charlotte Brontë complained that Austen "ruffles her reader by nothing vehement, disturbs him by nothing profound; the Passions are perfectly unknown to her"; D.H. Lawrence called her "a narrow-gutted spinster"; Joseph Conrad wondered: "What is there in her?"; Kingsley Amis argued that she habitually indulges those she should censure, and censures those she should indulge; while Mark Twain cheerfully commented that any library that didn't have a book by Jane Austen in it had the makings of being a good library.

Writing in 1949, the critic E.N. Hayes found the material Austen used in *Emma* "singularly confined", objecting to the fact that virtually all the fully developed characters belong to the upper middle class. There is no aristocracy; the lower middle class receive the same treatment, with young farmer Robert Martin scarcely making an appearance – he never speaks a word in the novel – and the poor are admitted only "to show that Emma is kindhearted".

Jane Austen is incapable of arriving at the conclusion that elegance, 'nice' manners, and simpering performances on the piano are stupid and wasteful. Her view is too narrow, her understanding too limited, her ethic too much bound to that of her class to understand the true nature of the lives of these people.

AUSTEN, LEAVIS AND TOLSTOY

The 20th-century critic F.R. Leavis famously asserted that a "Great Tradition" links Jane Austen with the other great exponents of the 19th-century novel, George Eliot, Henry James, Joseph Conrad and D.H. Lawrence. But in one respect, argues John Bayley, Leavis was wrong. We know where we are with the last four and what they believed; they make it abundantly clear. Our relationship with Austen is not like that: her attitude towards experience is more equivocal; it's much harder to define her attitudes or know what she thinks.

In one way we know her too well to be so coherently aware of her: and in another way we do not know her at all.

This is evident from the extraordinary variety of different critical responses to her work, especially to her

From this, and similar strictures, including the familiar one that Austen is incapable of writing about "the passion of love" because (in Hayes's almost certainly misguided view) she never experienced it, he proceeds to his damning conclusion:

> There is revealed in the book no attitude towards the major political, economic, psychological, or philosophical problems with which most novelists of importance since Richardson have more or less been concerned in their books. And if irony is the tone of *Emma*, the voice with which the author

last three novels, *Mansfield Park*, *Emma* and *Persuasion*. The real distinction, Bayley suggests, is not Leavis's one of a Great Tradition of the novel, but the distinction which puts Eliot and James on one side and Shakespeare, Austen and Tolstoy on the other.

The Victorian Thomas Babington Macaulay was the first critic to compare Austen with Shakespeare. They are certainly alike in being hard to pin down. Shakespeare had an uncanny ability to get inside his characters; Austen was the same. When Emma is rude to Miss Bates and then bitterly regrets it we feel we could easily have done the same thing, and we feel a kindred shame.

Whatever her image, Austen is no cosy old-fashioned peddler of Regency period pieces. In her breadth of outlook and the carefully defined nature of her world, says Bayley, the fictional writer she most resembles is Tolstoy. In his preface to the first, unpublished version of *War and Peace* in 1865, Tolstoy anticipated a possible charge that his view of Russian society was a limited one by writing that "the lives addresses her reader, it never carries any conception of the essential nature of man and society, which I take to be the ultimate subject of any good novel.

Of course Hayes is right that the world Austen evokes in *Emma* is strikingly ordinary, but as the distinguished critic and avowed "Janeite", John Bayley, points out, this very ordinariness is the key to its greatness. Austen "made up" Highbury, as all novelists make up places, "but it was the world she lived in and had to live in". She knew it as Emma

of officials, merchants, theological students and peasants do not interest me and are only half comprehensible to me". Tolstoy stuck to the people and the society he understood. So did Austen.

And Austen's fictional world, like Tolstoy's, seems complete because "both have the confidence of insiders. And this gives to [Austen's] world something of the Tolstoyan power of effortless expansion." Austen's characters can never escape society; nor (successfully) can Tolstoy's.

There is a big difference between the two, of course, as Bayley stresses.

It goes without saying that Jane Austen could not in the nature of things have performed Tolstoy's massive feat of sustaining a deep inner acceptance of society – with all it adds to the vitality and certainty of his characters – together with an external vision of it, and of [Anna Karenina and her lover Vronsky] when they have put themselves outside society. His ruthless comprehensiveness, his masculine freedom, could conjecture and continue to the bitter end where she could not ■

knows it by standing at the door of Ford's the draper. Though "much could not be hoped", still "she... was amused enough, quite enough still to stand at the door. A mind lively and at ease can do with seeing nothing, and can see nothing that does not answer"(27).*

Just as we are made to feel the reality of Highbury, so we are also made to see that Emma is part of it. As Bayley writes:

> Totally individual as she is, she is nonetheless a part of a community, and her existence depends upon the part she plays and will play in it. Her very mistakes arise from her dependence on it; her spirited sense of herself from her complete acceptance of the way it works.

Emma is constrained, even defined, by the society she belongs to. Her dreams, like her author's, do not go outside it; we feel its "enveloping intimacy", in Bayley's phrase. This gives the novel its power and endless fascination: we see in it the dilemmas and problems which we face in our own lives.

The reason we feel this "enveloping intimacy" so strongly is that the story is told almost entirely from the point of view of its heroine; we share her self-delusions, seeing almost everything through

*Throughout this book, the numbers in brackets refer to the chapters from which the quotations are taken.

her eyes and thoughts and reactions in a wonderfully flexible and sustained example of what is now called free indirect speech. While the story is told in the third person, by a narrator, the tone, expressions and thought patterns are those of Emma herself, so that we feel we are actually inside her. It is this use of free indirect speech which enables Austen to explore the psychology of the flawed but essentially good-natured Emma in such a convincing and profound way.

"We all have a better guide in ourselves, if we would attend to it, than any other person can be," says Fanny Price in *Mansfield Park* when the aspiring clergyman, Henry Crawford, calls her his moral guide. In her entertaining biography of Jane Austen, Claire Tomalin suggests Austen's "first flash of an idea for Emma" may have come when she wrote those words of Fanny's to Henry and "was struck by the comic possibility of an inner voice which turns out to be consistently wrong".

It is an intriguing thought, though it doesn't do justice to the subtlety of Austen's conception. For it is not true that Emma's inner voice is consistently wrong. The crucial word in Fanny Price's sentence – "We all have a better guide in ourselves, if we would attend to it…" – is that little word "if". Emma's inner voice is not faulty at all; it is perfectly sound. The problem is that she doesn't *attend* to it. The brilliance of Austen's narrative is that it makes clear from the beginning that underlying Emma's self-delusions is both the capacity for sound judgement and a deep interest in Mr Knightley. But for much of the novel Emma is a stranger to herself and to her heart, as ignorant of her own motives and innermost feelings as she is of other people's. She ignores her inner voice, and, thinking herself the most perceptive person in the world to which she belongs, is wrong about almost everyone and everything.

It is this division in Emma – her wilful blindness on the one hand, her cleverness and good nature on the other – which makes her such an engaging heroine, and, through the masterly use of free indirect speech, Austen shows us the workings not just of Emma's conscious mind but also of her subconscious mind.

There is, one guesses, little a modern behavioural psychologist could come up with which would shock Austen: the subconscious is a strange and fragile mechanism and she is very skilled at describing it; often we don't say what we mean because we don't know what we mean; we don't even properly understand our own thoughts. Because of this, the potential for causing pain and unhappiness is ever present. Mischief, even evil, can stem as easily from vanity, misapprehension and lack of self-knowledge as it can from malice. We know very little about other people, Austen suggests, and sometimes even less about ourselves. That, in essence, is what *Emma* is about.

Why do we fall for Emma?

Henry James described Jane Austen as an instinctive novelist whose effects can be explained as "part of her unconsciousness". It is as if she "fell-a-musing" over her work basket, he said, lapsed into "wool-gathering", and afterwards picked up "her dropped stitches" as "little master-strokes of imagination".

James is halfway there but only halfway. The unconsciousness we see unfolding in *Emma* is not Austen's but her heroine's; there is no reason to suppose that Austen wasn't perfectly aware of what she was doing. She had been experimenting with the use of free indirect speech at least since the earliest extant drafts of her fiction, and by the time she wrote *Emma* had developed it to a point where she could use it with extraordinary boldness and sophistication. The use of free indirect speech is the "most powerful innovation" in her fiction, says John Mullan in his lively book *What Matters in Jane Austen?*. We see the lack of self-knowledge of her central characters in the very voice of the narration.

In Emma she concentrates this effect as never before, narrating almost entirely from her heroine's point of view and bending reality to match her

Opposite: Gwyneth Paltrow as Emma in a 1996 film adaptation

preconceptions... Emma's self-delusions are not the subject of the narration, they are its very substance.

Indeed the heroine's presence in the novel is "so overweening", says Mullan, "that her absence, when it occurs, is a kind of shock". Occasionally the perspective shifts – in Chapter Five, for example, we have Mr Knightley talking confidentially to Mrs Weston about Emma's fate – but this is one of only four occasions when it does.[*] For the most part we "fully inhabit" her thoughts and therefore her delusions.

In writing about fiction, Henry James makes a distinction between "pictures" – which take us inside the mind of characters – and "scenes", which move the action forward. In *Emma* there is a rhythmic alternation between the two. Chapter 15, for example, is a "scene"; filled with dialogue and summaries of dialogue, it begins in the Westons' drawing room and ends with Mr Elton's violent proposal to Emma in the carriage, heated as he is with "Mr Weston's good wine" – imbibed to give himself Dutch courage. In the following chapter (a "picture") we are wholly within Emma's consciousness, as she conducts an internal dialogue

[*] The other three are all much later. There is a sudden switch to Mr Knightley's point of view to give us his suspicions about Frank Churchill; in the following chapter Mr Knightley and Mrs Elton discuss the strawberry party at Donwell; finally, there is the short conversation in which Mrs Weston tells Mr Weston about Emma's engagement.

with herself and agonises over what has happened: it is a reminder that Emma's view of what happened is more important than the events themselves.

As the American academic Wayne Booth points out in a justly admired analysis of Austen's narrative technique, she faced a tricky problem in writing *Emma*: in creating a heroine with serious faults – faults which threaten to do grave harm to other people – she was creating one her readers

AUSTEN'S OUTSPOKEN HEROINES

Some of Austen's female characters – Elinor Dashwood, Jane Bennet, Fanny Price, Anne Elliot – are gentle and passive. Austen's two favourite heroines, Elizabeth Bennet and Emma, are precisely the opposite. Both, argues Jan Fergus in her essay, "The Power of Women's Language and Laughter", are able to have equal and intimate relationships with their men (Mr Darcy and Mr Knightley) through their use of speech and laughter. "Unlike Darcy, Mr Knightley does not have to learn to be laughed at; Emma has long laughed at him..." In "Silent Women, Shrews, and Bluestockings", another feminist critic, Jocelyn Harris, argues that in allowing her women characters to speak so cleverly Austen subverts "misogynist constructions of women" who "have always been discouraged from knowing, speaking, and writing".

In *Emma*, says Harris, the heroine's openness is preferable to Jane Fairfax's reserve, even if Emma "says too much too often". She, might not "much like". Yet if her readers failed to like, even love, the heroine, the novel would fail, and the conclusion, her happy and deserved marriage to Mr Knightley, would seem implausible and unacceptable.

Seen from the outside Emma could easily come across as quite unpleasant. She attempts to manipulate Harriet not from an excess of kindness but from a desire for power and admiration. She flirts with Frank Churchill out of vanity and

---

"like Elizabeth Bennet, speaks too freely because her father's power is weak". But Austen shields these two outspoken, intelligent heroines from being labelled shrews or bluestockings by the use of free indirect speech – so we sometimes find them thinking uncharitable thoughts which they are too tactful to express out loud.

Austen was highly conscious of the effect of gender on language. Anne Elliot in *Persuasion* comments that "men have every advantage of us in telling their story. Education has been theirs in so much higher a degree." It is a point echoed by Thomas Hardy in *Far From the Madding Crowd*, when his heroine, Bathsheba Everdene, thinks that "it is difficult for a woman to define her feelings in language which is chiefly made by men to express theirs". In her famous feminist polemic, *A Room of One's Own*, Virginia Woolf suggests in 1929 that men tend to be more self-confident than women because society is structured to develop and enhance their confidence. Indeed the novel itself, she argues, arose as a direct result of women's need to find a form with which to reconstruct themselves in a changing society ∎

irresponsibility. She mistreats Jane Fairfax because of Jane's good qualities.

We only have to imagine how Emma's actions would be described by Jane Fairfax, for most of the narrative, or by Robert Martin, to realise how unsympathetic a character Emma might be made to seem, and because we see almost everything through Emma's eyes it is important not just that we understand her faults, but that we are quickly aware of her worth. She is carefully "placed" for us in the famous early paragraphs of the novel:

> *Emma Woodhouse, handsome, clever, and rich, with a comfortable home and happy disposition, seemed to unite some of the best blessings of existence; and had lived very nearly twenty-one years in the world with very little to distress or vex her. (1)*

The word "seemed" in this highly charged first sentence is important: it is a key word in the novel – appearing in one form or another (seems/seeming) more than 70 times – and it is immediately reinforced by more directly stated reservations.

> *The real evils of Emma's situation were the power of having rather too much her own way, and a disposition to think a little too well of herself; these were the disadvantages which*

threatened alloy to her many enjoyments.
The danger, however, was at present so
unperceived, that they did not by any means
rank as misfortunes with her.

None of this, as Wayne Booth points out, could have been said by Emma herself, yet we need to know it before we can be allowed to see the world

---

FREE INDIRECT SPEECH

One does not automatically think of Jane Austen as an innovative novelist – like, for example, James Joyce who drastically rewrote the rules of writing modernist fiction. But Austen is credited with one major narrative device which has proved immensely useful and interesting to her novel-writing successors. It has been labelled "Free Indirect Speech" (or "Style" or "Discourse").

It was Freud (pictured left) who said that he "discovered" nothing. Psychoanalysis merely codified and systematised what the great writers of literature had discovered before he came along. It was in the 1920s, a century after Austen died, that the linguist Otto Jesperson gave Free Indirect Speech (FIS) its rather off-putting name.

What is FIS? A useful illustration can be found in drama. In a play like Shakespeare's *Othello* major characters, such as Iago and the hero, have distinctive styles of speech (the hero's majestic utterance has been called "the Othello music"). Yet both of them speak in a way which is recognisably "Shakespearian". Their through her eyes. Once we know it we are in a position to see the ironic barbs directed at Emma which the narrator intends us to see. Take the moment we are introduced to Harriet:

Emma was not struck by any thing remarkably clever in Miss Smith's conversation, but she found her altogether very engaging – not

language is a mix of them, and of their creator.

All of us, whether creative writers or not, have our own ways of speaking – as distinctive as our fingerprints. Throughout her career Jane Austen writes like Jane Austen. Yet she constantly attempts to break out into the minds, lives, and speech patterns of others. FIS allows her narrative to slip inside the thought processes – not necessarily wholly verbalised – of Emma Woodhouse, and gives the reader a vivid sense of "listening" to Austen while, at the same time, "being" Emma – or, at least, dipping inside her ever-active mind. It is a technique which not only demands great

skill from the writer, but reciprocal skill from the reader. It is not the least aspect of Austen's greatness that she makes us cleverer readers. We close *Emma* better equipped – trained, one might say – to respond to fiction.

Austen's successors learned from her work as well as merely enjoying it. Of her successors, Virginia Woolf (a dyed-in-the-wool Austenite), was a virtuoso performer on the FIS instrument – evolving it into what has been called "Stream of Consciousness". Take the following passage from *Mrs Dalloway* (the heroine, Clarissa, is walking from Westminster to Bond Street in London, on a fine June morning). Whose

*inconveniently shy, not unwilling to talk – and
yet so far from pushing, shewing so proper and
becoming a deference, and so artlessly impressed
by the appearance of every thing in so superior a
style to what she had been used to, that she must
have good sense and deserve encouragement.
Encouragement should be given. Those soft blue
eyes... should not be wasted on the inferior
society of Highbury. (3)*

voice(s) does the reader "hear"?

For having lived in Westminster – how many years now? over twenty, – one feels even in the midst of the traffic, or waking at night, Clarissa was positive, a particular hush, or solemnity; an indescribable pause; a suspense (but that might be her heart, affected, they said, by influenza) before Big Ben strikes. There! Out it boomed. First a warning, musical; then the hour, irrevocable. The leaden circles dissolved in the air. Such fools we are, she thought, crossing Victoria Street.

The last remark about "crossing Victoria Street" is clearly authorial. We hear Woolf telling us something. The rest is Clarissa Dalloway. But would a middle-aged, Conservative politician's wife come up with that wonderful metaphor about leaden circles dissolving in the air? There is a tang of Woolf among the Dalloway here. Her "stain" we may say, irremovably there in the fabric of the narrative.

Emma is an immensely pleasurable novel. A major part of the pleasure it yields-- rather like being at a fine concert – is hearing the subtle mix of vocalisation in the text. It is, we may say, a novel which should be "listened to" carefully ∎

This passage brilliantly catches the way Emma thinks and her chronic confusion of appearance and reality. She carries on in the same vein, giving herself away with every word as she pours out her own beneficence and general value. Harriet's past friends, "though very good sort of people, must be doing her harm", thinks Emma. Without knowing them, she concludes that they "must be coarse and unpolished, and very unfit to be the intimates of a girl who wanted only a little more knowledge and elegance to be quite perfect".

And Emma finishes with a burst of unmitigated egotism.

> *She would notice her; she would improve her; she would detach her from her very bad acquaintance, and introduce her into good society; she would form her opinions and manners. It would be interesting, and certainly a very kind undertaking; highly becoming her own situation in life, her leisure, and powers. (3)*

It would be difficult for us to see the ironies in all this, and to appreciate the monstrousness of what Emma is planning – as she lists all the possible egoistical uses she has for Harriet under the guise of services she will perform for her – unless the narrator had set out her heroine's situation first with great care. But because we know of the potential "evils" facing Emma we are on our guard and in a position to appreciate the irony. Free indirect speech is an intrinsically ironic method: we see from two different perspectives at the same time. We are both inside and outside Emma's mind during the novel, as, in life, we are both inside and outside our own minds. Sometimes we know what we're about, sometimes not; the inadequacy of our own vision of things – as much as the inadequacies of Emma's – is the constant target of Austen's irony.

But while Austen makes us aware of Emma's faults, she never neglects to impress on us her overriding good qualities: her energy, her cleverness, her "eager laughing warmth", her capacity for tenderness and affection. Her kindness is often quietly alluded to: she is generous to the poor, and devotedly looks after her hypochondriac father (while ensuring that his visitors are properly fed).

We are constantly drawn to Emma's wit and style. Here are four characteristic passages:

> *"Never mind, Harriet, I shall not be a poor old maid; it is poverty only which makes celibacy contemptible to a generous public!" (10)*

> *Emma was sorry; to have to pay civilities to a person she did not like through three long*

months! – to be always doing more than she
wished and less than she ought! (20)

"I do not know whether it ought to be so, but
certainly silly things do cease to be silly if they
are done by sensible people in an impudent way.
Wickedness is always wickedness, but folly is not
always folly." (26)

"Oh! I always deserve the best treatment,
because I never put up with any other..." (54)

The funniest of Austen's heroines, Emma endears
herself to us because of her capacity for laughter,
not least at herself. When Mr Knightley says at
the Westons' ball that he will leave her to "her
reflections", she replies wittily: "Can you trust me
to those little flatterers?" In Chapter Ten, when
she and Harriet visit an impoverished family in
Highbury, she is at pains to disabuse us of the
notion that she is truly altruistic:

"These are the sights, Harriet, to do one good.
How trifling they make everything else appear! –
I feel now as if I could think of nothing but these
poor creatures all the rest of the day; and, yet,
who can say how soon it may all vanish from my
mind?" (10)

The self-mockery in this is yet another reminder

that despite the wilful blindness and lack of humility she is far from incapable of self-knowledge and has a perfectly sound inner voice. For all her faults we cannot help but be struck by what the narrator calls her "wonderful velocity of thought"; she has a quick, flexible mind; she is never dull.

Emma is redeemed, too, by her fondness for Mr Knightley – severe as he often is with her. She may not realise she loves him, but she is constantly aware of him; she notices when he comes into a room; she hates being criticised by him. When he rebukes her for making Harriet refuse Robert Martin, for example, we know he's right. But Emma?

Emma made no answer, and tried to look cheerfully unconcerned, but was really feeling uncomfortable, and wanting him very much to be gone. She did not repent of what she had done; still thought herself a better judge of such a point of female right and refinement than he could be; but yet she had a sort of habitual respect for his judgement in general, which made her dislike having it so loudly against her; and to have him sitting just opposite to her in angry state, was very disagreeable. (8)

The narrative voice in *Emma* is overwhelmingly Emma's voice – youthful, confident, presumptive, witty, dogmatic, commanding, assured – but through the way Austen controls the point of view we are enabled to see (as she cannot) her faults and condemn them while at the same time retaining our sympathy for the wayward heroine. The narration's "way of *saying* is constantly both mimicking, and distancing itself from, the character's way of *seeing*", writes D.A. Miller in *Jane Austen or The Secret of Style*. Our emotional responses echo Emma's; we feel her anxiety and shame; and we tolerate her faults in the same way we tolerate our own.

What need in Emma does Harriet satisfy?

Good mothers are few and far between in Jane Austen. Her heroines, with the exception of Catherine Morland, lack strong, sensible mothers to guide them: Elizabeth Bennet's in *Pride and Prejudice* is foolish and vulgar, Mrs Dashwood in *Sense and Sensibility* impractical and of little help to Elinor; Fanny's mother in *Mansfield Park* is a slattern; Anne Elliot's in *Persuasion*, like Emma's, died during the heroine's childhood.

In the absence of her mother, Emma has been brought up by her weak, fretful and self-centred father. Miss Taylor, her governess, has been no substitute for a mother or even an older sister, acting more like a servile playmate to Emma. Her efforts at tutoring have not been successful, as the ignored reading lists of her pupil attest. Nor is Miss Taylor – the name hints at a "low" background in "trade" – sensible to encourage Emma's patronage of Harriet, failing to see that her charge could cause great misery to an unprotected girl.

Restless and undisciplined, Emma has little to occupy her, and for a girl with such natural "velocity of thought" this is part of the problem. In his astute essay on "Emma 'The Match-Maker'",

HARRIET'S BLOOM

We are told that Harriet is possessed of the feminine "beauty" Emma particularly admires. She is "short, plump and fair, with a fine bloom". That last word is peculiarly Austenish and comes up in all the novels, most prominently in the last complete work, *Persuasion*, in which the question of whether Anne Elliot is losing her bloom is central. We may assume that Emma (six years younger than Anne) is radiantly blooming (the term "brilliant" is applied to her). Jane Fairfax is not blooming – her face is suspiciously pallid. So much so that Mr Knightley, suspecting vitaminosis (a chronic condition in the 19th century when fruit and vegetables were seasonal), gives the Bateses his precious last store of apples. Jane's pallor, of course, has another source, but Mr Knightley's gift of what will be withered fruit is well meant and well observed ∎

the late 20th-century critic Tony Tanner quotes
from a book called *Sex and Character* by Otto
Weininger. Published in 1903, this is in many ways
a misogynistic treatise but it makes, in extreme
form, a central point relevant to Emma's position.
After talking of the immeasurable superiority of
men, Weininger asks: "But has woman no meaning
at all? Has she no general purpose in the scheme
of the world? Has she not a destiny; and, in spite of
all her senselessness and emptiness, a significance
in the universe?" His answer is firm and clear. "It is
from nothing less than the phenomenon of match-
making from which we may be able to infer most
correctly the real nature of women." In Weininger's
view, match-making "is the most common
characteristic of the human female", the key to

WOMEN CONFINED

Austen was acutely
conscious of the limitations
facing women. The first half
of *Pride and Prejudice*
consists essentially of
women waiting for men and
scheming about them. In
Persuasion, Anne Elliot

accurately reflects the world
19th-century girls lived in
when she remarks to
Captain Harville:

> "We cannot help ourselves.
> We live at home, quiet,
> confined, and our feelings
> prey upon us. You [men]
> are forced to exertion. You
> have a profession, pursuits,
> business of some sort or
> other, to take you back into
> the world..." (23)

In *Emma*, says the critic
John Wiltshire, women are

"woman's nature". Femaleness is "identical with pairing".

Weininger's views, however unfashionable today, are uncomfortably reflective of the world of *Emma*: she is, from the beginning, a matchmaker. In the very first chapter she claims credit for the match between Miss Taylor and Mr Weston ("It is a matter of joy... that I made the match myself...") and though Mr Knightley dismisses the claim – thinking they would marry was just "a lucky guess" on Emma's part, he says – her father pleads with her to make no more matches. Emma, however, merrily replies: "I promise to make none for myself, papa; but I must, indeed, for other people. It is the greatest amusement in the world!" Note that "must", as Tony Tanner says: it is "an imperative"

more or less limited to drawing rooms, but men can visit their neighbours at all hours and even go off to London for a haircut (as Frank Churchill does). Jane Fairfax is subjected to a neighbourly inquisition when caught walking in the rain to the local post office on the chance of hearing from her beloved, while Mr Knightley is free to ride through the rain all the way from London. Space in the novel, says Wiltshire, is thus "gendered": men travel; women are shut in, and their "imprisonment is associated with deprivation, with energies and powers perverted in their application, and events, balls and outings are linked with the arousal and satisfaction of desires". Emma herself, despite her £30,000 a year, has never been to London and, when the story starts, hasn't even visited Mr Knightley's home, Donwell Abbey, for two years ∎

of her self-pleasing, ungoverned wilfulness.

Are there also hints in the novel of impulses which are never quite explored and of which Emma herself is unaware? Janet Todd argues that because of the role she has played at Hartfield, with one hopeless parent and the pliable Miss Taylor, she is essentially still a spoilt child who has not had to enter the adult world of adult emotion:

> Having played adored wife – or rather husband – to her weak and coercive father since her mother's early death, she has come to assume that she lacks the qualities more virile men want.

It may well have been a shock to Emma's adolescence when her elder sister, Isabella, was chosen by Mr Knightley's clever younger brother, John. "Along with the fecund, sweet and limited Isabella and the obliging governess, the simple Harriet seems what men desire."

From a mixture of fear and emotional immaturity Emma, in her schoolgirlish way, acts through others, using them to fulfil her emotional needs and as surrogates for her guarded self. "I know that such a girl as Harriet is exactly what every man delights in – what at once bewitches his senses and satisfies his judgement," she tells Mr Knightley. Harriet, to Emma, is a fantasy sexual object, a substitute of Emma's making who, in Tony Tanner's words, will engage in all the potentially dangerous male-female (i.e. sexual – we can say it even if Jane Austen does not think it necessary to spell it out) relationships which might amuse or distract Emma (*something* has to distract her) and which she can enjoy vicariously.

As the critic Marvin Mudrick has suggested (implausibly, not to say outrageously, to many dyed-in-the-wool Janeites), there may even be an element of "inadmissible homo-erotic love" in Emma's feelings for Harriet – she has, after all, been more like a husband than a daughter to her father and she demands from Harriet absolute affection, forcing her at one point to declare: "I would not give up the pleasure and honour of being intimate with you for any thing in the world." She has made Harriet choose her over a man and become dependent on her, a fate which, as Mr Knightley says, Mrs Weston was lucky to avoid.*

Is Emma a snob?

In taking up a parlour boarder in Mrs Goddard's village school, known to be of illegitimate birth, Emma chooses a protégée she can do what she

* "Was Jane Austen Gay?" inquired the lesbian-feminist critic Terry Castle, in 1995, in the wake of the revelation that Jane Austen shared a bed with her (similarly unmarried) sister Cassandra.

likes with; a pretty nobody who will satisfy her whims. There is a snag: Harriet has already formed an attachment of sorts with a young farmer, Robert Martin. On discovering this, Emma typically tries to force the issue by putting Harriet in a position where she will have to choose between them. She tells Harriet that she (Emma) cannot possibly associate with anyone of Robert Martin's class:

> *"The yeomanry are precisely the order of people with whom I feel I can have nothing to do. A degree or two lower, and a creditable appearance might interest me; I might hope to be useful to their families in some way or other. But a farmer can need none of my help, and is therefore in one sense as much above my notice as in every other he is below it." (4)*

Lionel Trilling, perhaps the most influential American critic of the 20th century, argues that Emma is "a dreadful snob". It is Emma's snobbery, he says, that causes her to make a terrible mistake: in the passage quoted above she expresses "a principled social contempt" for the very group in society that had long been regarded as the backbone of the country and its mainstay in times of trouble.

If Emma is really doing that, she is indeed a snob and a culpable snob at that. Being aware of one's position in society, however, is not the same as being a snob. However offensive to modern democratic sensibilities Emma's attitude may be, she is not denigrating the yeomanry; she is simply describing, bluntly, the way things are – or were.

In a 1985 essay, "Lionel Trilling and *Emma*: A Reconsideration", Paul Pickrel argues that Trilling has simply misread Austen's novel. Whatever we think of her heroine, we shouldn't take what she says at face value. We have, as it were, to read *through* her to what lies behind. Take, for example, the passage later in the narrative when it is suggested to Emma that Mr Knightley might marry Jane Fairfax: Emma is outraged on behalf of little Henry, her nephew; she thinks he should inherit Donwell, and if Mr Knightley remains a bachelor, that is what will happen; the estate will go to the oldest son of Mr Knightley's brother and Emma's sister. But if Mr Knightley marries, then he is likely to produce an heir of his own and little Henry will be left estate-less.

Now if Emma is being truthful about her motives here then she must be, in Pickrel's words, "a most reprehensibly avaricious young woman to become so upset at the prospect of a valuable piece of property escaping the clutches of her nephew". But she is not being truthful; as so often, she is deluding herself. For all her faults, Emma is not mean. Her concern (although she cannot admit it, even to herself) is not with who gets Donwell, but with who gets Mr Knightley. Her outcry on behalf of young Henry is nothing more than an attempt to defend her own interests. She doesn't want Jane Fairfax to marry Mr Knightley because she is in love with him herself, but she doesn't yet know this, so she assumes her anxiety about the possible match stems from something else, and avarice on behalf of little Henry is the best she can come up with. In the end, when she is about to marry Mr Knightley, we are told she is "never struck with any sense of injury to her nephew Henry". Once she knows herself better, the alleged motive of avarice becomes irrelevant.

"Emma is no snob," says Pickrel.

> She sometimes gives snobbish motives for her actions but always, I believe, for one of three reasons: she does not know her real motives, or she is ashamed of them, or she has some strategic reason for disguising them.

In the case of her snobbish remarks about Robert Martin, she has a very good "strategic reason" to disguise her motives. She wants to drive a wedge between him and Harriet so she can have Harriet to herself, and, with no good wedge to hand, Mr Martin's social position will have to serve, even if Emma is on shaky ground when she draws attention to it. Mr Martin, after all, could hardly be a more suitable match for a girl in Harriet's position. Marilyn Butler compares his character to Mr Knightley's, calling him Mr Knightley's "wholly silent alter ego" – silent because he "acts, and simply is, with the solidity that comes from well-defined involvement with a physical world". His financial circumstances are good and likely to improve; his family is fond of Harriet and he himself is devoted to her. When Harriet visited the family the previous summer, we are told, Martin went "three miles round" to gather walnuts for her, and one evening he had the shepherd's boy come and sing for her – charming, delicate attentions unmatched by any other suitor in Austen's work. Moreover he is at least as respectable as Harriet, probably more so. Harriet, however, is too stupid to see through her patroness's flimsy argument.

Even Emma herself is aware of its flimsiness.* She is forced to recognise that Martin's letter of proposal to Harriet is excellent:

> *...as a composition it would not have disgraced a gentleman; the language, though plain, was strong and unaffected... [It] expressed good sense, warm attachment, liberality, propriety, even delicacy of feeling. (7)*

*John Mullan says the plot of *Emma* depends on Martin's decision to propose in writing. "This gives the weak-minded Harriet the opportunity to go to Emma for advice..." Had he made his proposal in person he would almost certainly have won her round.

Emma's recognition of the merits of Martin's letter measures the extent to which, as Kathleen Parkinson puts it, "she represses her own discriminating intelligence in favour of wilful fantasies of love". She simply shuts out facts she doesn't want to acknowledge. "He will be a completely gross vulgar farmer – totally inattentive to appearances, and thinking of nothing but profit and loss," she tells Harriet in Chapter Four. Her contempt for farmers is later echoed by a seeming contempt for lawyers: "Oh! No, I could not endure William Cox – a pert young lawyer," she says in Chapter 16 when considering other potential suitors for Harriet. And yet the man she ends up

EMMA'S FEAR OF SEX

It is reasonable to assume that at a level which she is not inclined to investigate Emma is terrified by sex, and nervous about marriage. She has, for example, been present at her sister Isabella's five lyings-in. (Early 19th-century pregnancy and childbirth were not easy for the women who underwent it.) Emma has witnessed, too, what motherhood and marriage has done to her sister – turned her into a dull woman, garrulous but incapable of saying anything of the slightest interest. Even her bearish husband, John, finds her a bore and sees no reason (as the Christmas celebrations at Hartfield testify) to disguise his impatience. And why did a sharp fellow like John marrying is a farmer (and one who broods a lot about profit and loss), while his brother is a lawyer.

In her determination to have her own way Emma resembles her father, who uses his own feebleness to tyrannise over those around him. Weak, domineering and selfish, her father "diminishes everything around him", as Janet Todd puts it. The half-glass of wine offered to Mrs Goddard in his house becomes a small half and is then diluted with water. And Emma's world is contracted too, until she is "almost housebound". She cannot even walk the half-mile across the Highbury common to Randall's on her own

Knightley marry Isabella in the first place? Because, as the older sister, she probably had even more than Emma's £30,000 to endow her husband with.

The Knightleys are hard up – scarcely able to keep up the Donwell estate. And by the English laws of primogeniture the bachelor second son, John Knightley, had a bleak outlook. With Isabella's fortune, however, he can buy into a London law firm and afford his fine house in Brunswick Square.

Isabella's destiny is to breed. Who can blame Emma for looking askance at what marriage holds – even for a woman who is "handsome, clever, and rich"?

Emma's fear of sex is also hinted at in her ignorance of the seaside. She has never even seen the sea, unlike her marriage-hating father, who observes: "the sea is very rarely of use to any body. I am sure it almost killed me once." There are without causing her father anxiety – in striking contrast to Jane Fairfax who, to Emma's amazement, walks from Donwell to Highbury alone. Mr Woodhouse believes marriages are "silly things, and break up one's family circle grievously". It is hard to see how a family circle could exist at all without marriage but, as Tony Tanner puts it,

> this moribund patriarch is a comic-serious example of the type of male who would indeed bring his society – any society – to a stop. He is the weak emasculate voice of definitive negations and terminations. He is a (barely) living embodiment of his society's entropic tendencies.

frequent suggestions in Austen, John Mullan reminds us, that the seaside is a place of licence where the usual restraints don't apply. Sometimes it is dangerous. In *Pride and Prejudice* Lydia falls prey to Wickham's seducing wiles in Brighton, and the near-seduction of Darcy's sister also happens by the sea. "In Austen's novels, seaside resorts are places for flirtations and engagements, attachments and elopements, love and sex."

While Emma is contriving her fantasy courtship of Harriet by Mr Elton, a "true amour" (between Frank and Jane) is being pursued on the Dorset coast. "Emma's ignorance of what it might be like by the sea takes on an added significance. She does indeed know nothing of this zone of love." It will be by the sea, finally, "that she and Mr Knightley begin a sexual relationship" – once engaged, they agree on a honeymoon by the seaside ∎

Emma's own fearfulness is, in a way, a reflection of her father's; like him, she wants to control everyone and everything around her. The combination is a dangerous one, and by interfering in Harriet's life and warning her off Robert Martin she poses a real threat to the future of a naïve 17-year-old. But it is too simplistic to say snobbishness causes her to sideline Robert Martin: she wants Harriet to herself and, like a child, will say anything to keep her. In her childishness, she is like her father, who, in Janet Todd's words, is "never able to suppose that other people could feel differently from himself".

How much of a setback to Emma is her humiliation by Mr Elton?

Mr Elton and Augusta Hawkins, the woman he eventually marries, are the only two entirely unsympathetic characters in the novel. Other than good looks – he is "a pretty young man" – and a university education (the only one in Highbury), Mr Elton has little to recommend him, at least in Emma's savage eyes. (The teachers and girls in Mrs Goddard's establishment adore him, and make copies of his sermons.) Though a minister, he seems entirely lacking in genuine Christian feelings; his behaviour is never anything other than selfish. In his courting of Emma, he is as blind as she is and being older (26), with less excuse; while she misinterprets his advances as being made to Harriet, he fails to understand her response and, as she eventually realises, his very lack of "elegancy of mind" and "talent" prevents him from understanding that Emma would never dream of marrying him. Later, when he declines, brutally, to dance with Harriet at the ball (Chapter 38) he amply demonstrates his lack of compassion, an impression reinforced by his complicity with his wife in snubbing her: "smiles of high glee passed between him [and Mrs Elton]".

His unsuitability for a sacred calling and general lack of worth are further evidenced by his choice of wife – one of the many ironies of the novel is that Emma makes a better choice for him in Harriet than he does for himself. Augusta Hawkins may bring £10,000 to the marriage, but she is a ridiculous figure with her barouche-landau, *caro sposo* – or, as she mispronounces it, "cara sposo" – and boasting of her brother-in-law's property, Maple Grove. Mr Elton's decision to marry her leads us to make an even harsher judgement of his character.

Nor does he seem much interested in his less fortunate parishioners. When Emma and Harriet visit a poor neighbourhood in Highbury we are told

that Emma "understood their ways" and "entered into their troubles with ready sympathy". Later, however, the ladies bump into Mr Elton, whose reaction makes us question his priorities:

> *The wants and sufferings of the poor family... were the first subject on meeting. He had been going to call on them. His visit he would now defer. (10)*

The awfulness of Mr Elton highlights the extent of Emma's blindness. She sees that he lacks true gentility: she knows his determination "to sigh and languish, and study for compliments" is pure affectation, and would be intolerable if directed at herself. She even admits to herself that he is "almost too gallant" to be really in love. When Emma paints a portrait of Harriet for Mr Elton, she knows that Mr Elton's verdict – "a most perfect resemblance in every feature" – is not true, and that Mr Knightley's "You have made her too tall" is more accurate. (The narrator has already guided our thinking on Emma's artistic talents with typical irony: "There was merit in every drawing – in the least finished perhaps the most.")

This portrait-judging scene amusingly underlines the novel's preoccupation with the limits of individual perception. Mr Elton can see no fault because he is besotted with the artist; Mrs Weston's view – that Emma has "improved"

Harriet's eyebrows and lashes – reflects her idea that Emma is good for Harriet; while Mr Knightley's indicates his belief that Harriet has been elevated above her station. Mr Woodhouse, for his part, can only think of Harriet's health: she "seems to be sitting out of doors, with only a little shawl over her shoulders – and it makes one think she must catch cold".

When Mr Elton finally proposes, Emma is horrified. But Austen is careful to show us that it is very much her fault; both Knightley brothers warn her that Mr Elton is not serious about Harriet, with John Knightley hitting on the truth when he says to Emma that Mr Elton "seems to have a great deal of good-will towards you".

MR WOODHOUSE'S WEALTH

Deirdre le Faye, who has given the matter critical thought, asks, pertinently, where does Mr Woodhouse's wealth come from? Le Faye's speculation is that it must originally have come from agricultural land, which has been sold off (farms drew in a high price in the early Napoleonic War period – something that Marilyn Butler points to, in *Jane Austen and the War of Ideas*). All that is left, apart from Mr Woodhouse's substantial bank account, is Hartfield, the house at the centre of all the fields the family once owned. But since he only has daughters, and the money will be lost in dowry, it is of less consequence than if he had had a male heir ∎

Emma's reply to this is a marvellous piece of anticipatory dramatic irony in which, as often, she attributes to others characteristics and ways of thinking which really apply to herself:

> "I thank you; but I assure you that you are quite mistaken. Mr Elton and I are very good friends, and nothing more"; and she walked on, amusing herself in the consideration of the blunders which often arise from a partial knowledge of circumstances... (13)

But unlike Mr Elton, who is doomed forever to be

> proud, assuming, conceited; very full of his own claims, and little concerned with the feelings of others... (16)

Emma has the capacity to learn from her mistake.

> The first error and the worst lay at her door. It was foolish, it was wrong, to take so active a part in bringing any two people together... She was quite concerned and ashamed, and resolved to do such things no more.

But though she learns a lesson, and knows herself a little better now, she is by no means cured; she continues to delude herself that people will act as she imagines them doing and to see others as little more than extensions of her own ego.

She would gladly have submitted to feel yet more mistaken – more in error – more disgraced by mis-judgement, than she actually was, could the effects of her blunders have been confined to herself.

In this very subtle passage, says John Mullan, "we can hear [Emma's] capacity for self-delusion beginning to reassert itself even in the train of apparent self-condemnation:

"gladly have submitted" is her turn of phrase or turn of thought, as she tells herself that she would be happy to be "disgraced" if only Harriet were to escape the consequences of her errors. She acknowledges that she has "blundered most dreadfully", yet she does so in a passage where most of her delusions remain intact.

After this first humiliation, we are told, Emma "got up on the morrow more disposed for comfort than she had gone to bed..." Despite the misery she has caused Harriet, a good night's rest – and the brushing of her hair by her maidservant – restores her spirits. Significantly, when she is humiliated for the second time, later in the novel, there is no such easy cure.

Is Mr Knightley right about Frank Churchill?

It has been said that there are no bad people in *Emma*; only bad acts. The nearest the novel has to a villain is Frank Churchill: repeatedly mentioned in the first volume, he makes his appearance in the second, as does his secret fiancée, Jane Fairfax.

All Jane Austen's villains are, in a sense, actors: they are masters, says Robin Gilmour in *The Idea of the Gentleman in the Victoran Novel*, of what Lord Chesterfield called "those lesser talents, of an engaging, insinuating manner, an easy good breeding, a genteel behaviour and address". Frank Churchill is not a shameless seducer like Wickham in *Pride and Prejudice* or Willoughby in *Sense and Sensibility*, but he may also fit Chesterfield's description.

How harshly should we judge Frank? When he writes to his father making excuses for not visiting Highbury, Mr Knightley's condemnation is quick, and severe.

Letters are very important in *Emma*, as are the ways in which they are interpreted. Emma is wilfully myopic in her reading of Robert Martin's plain, unadorned love letter. Now, when Frank's letter is read at Randall's, it is Mr Knightley's turn to be disparaging. "He can sit down and write a

Opposite: Ewan McGregor as Frank Churchill in the 1996 film

fine flourishing letter," Mr Knightley says, "full of professions and falsehoods, and persuade himself that he has hit upon the very best method in the world of preserving peace at home and preventing his father's having any right to complain. His letters disgust me." He goes on to make a definitive moral judgement.

"No, Emma, your amiable young man can be amiable only in French, not in English. He may

THE BAROUCHE-LANDAU

In *Emma*, a "carriage" can refer to any horse-drawn conveyance – whether gig, coach, stagecoach or barouche. Travel by "carriages" is the accepted and expected mode of transport for those of social standing. When Mr Knightley arrives at the Coles' party in his own carriage – since he keeps no horses, most of his travel across Highbury happens on foot – Emma is thoroughly approving; "this is coming as you should – like a gentleman".

But as the only model to be named, and named repeatedly, the barouche-landau becomes a mark of Mrs Elton's quite exceptional vulgarity. A fairly large vehicle – we are told it "holds four perfectly" – it was a modern invention at the time of Austen's writing. Edward Ratcliffe ("Transports of Delight: How Jane Austen's characters got around") *be very 'aimable', have very good manners, and be very agreeable; but he can have no English delicacy towards the feelings of other people; nothing really amiable about him." (18)*

This seems extreme, and it is. Mr Knightley's opinion that Frank is probably "proud, luxurious and selfish" is clearly biased, not just because there is an instinctive antipathy between them – they are opposites – but because Mr Knightley is jealous:

notes that, while a barouche had a collapsing hood over the back passenger seats, "the barouche-landau top covers the entire passenger area when raised and is arranged in two parts; the front part folds forward, the back part folds to the rear".

An appendix to Chapman's 1934 edition of *Mansfield Park* is relevant:

For barouche-landau, Mr. W. H. Helm refers me to the Morning Post, 5 Jan. 1804, where it is announced that "Mr. Buxton, the celebrated whip, has just launched a newfangled machine, a kind of nondescript. It is

described by the inventor to be the due medium between a landau and a barouche, but all who have seen it say it more resembles a fish-cart or a music-caravan."

One can picture the reaction had such a vehicle ever made its appearance amidst the unfashionable traffic of Highbury. Even at a permanent remove, Mrs Elton hopes that it will lend credence to her social aspirations. The reality, of course, is that both she and the barouche-landau cast a quite different impression; that of an ostentatious intrusion, in poor taste ∎

he fears Emma is attracted to the idea of Frank Churchill and, though he isn't yet conscious of it, he is in love with Emma himself. Mr Knightley's over-reaction makes the reader wonder about his motives, especially as he is so measured and sensible on other subjects: he has never met Frank Churchill and knows little about him, far too little to make such a stern judgement; yet he is determined to find fault at every opportunity, condemning him for passing time in Weymouth – "one of the idlest haunts in the kingdom"* – even, later, censuring Frank's handwriting as effeminate and, finally, and absurdly, calling him an "Absolute scoundrel!" Emma is right in her opinion that he is being "illiberal":

> *to take a dislike to a young man, only because he appeared to be of a different disposition from himself, was unworthy of the real liberality of mind which she was always used to acknowledge in him; for with all the high opinion of himself, which she had often laid to his charge, she had never before for a moment supposed it could make him unjust to the merit of another. (18)*

When Emma accuses Mr Knightley of being

* In fact, as John Mullan points out, Weymouth was a respectable resort – more so than Brighton, where Lydia is seduced by Wickham in *Pride and Prejudice*. It was a favourite of George III and his family; Knightley's disapproval of it is just another symptom of his jealousy.

"illiberal" she implies that he is failing to live up to his own high moral standards. Frank, after all, has good qualities as well as bad: he can be gracious and pleasant. He mends Mrs Bates's spectacles for her and, when he first arrives in Highbury, begs his father to show him over the house in which he (Mr Weston) has lived so long; then, "on recollecting that an old woman who had nursed him was still living, walked in quest of her cottage from one end of the street to the other" (20).

There is, nevertheless, some truth in Mr Knightley's verdict. Frank is a shameless manipulator who deceives everyone. We see him entirely from the outside, but in handling his secret engagement with Jane, he seems, as John Wiltshire says, to be both uneasy with the game he is forced into and to find the deception entertaining. Sly and impetuous, he strains against the restrictions of secrecy while at the same time enjoying the opportunities for mischief it presents. Mr Woodhouse, in perhaps his most perceptive judgement in the novel, sees through him at once. "Do not tell his father," the old man says to Emma after Frank has paid a visit, "but that young man is not quite the thing. He has been opening the doors very often this evening, and keeping them open very inconsiderately. He does not think of the draught. I do not mean to set you against him, but indeed he is not quite the thing!" (29).

But while Frank may not be "quite the thing",

the novel suggests an alternative way of seeing him to Mr Woodhouse's and Mr Knightley's. Frank is a great believer in fresh air. The thought of him opening windows at the ball in Highbury provokes Mr Woodhouse into something near panic.

"Open the windows!... Nobody could be so imprudent! I never heard of such a thing. Dancing with open windows! I am sure neither your father nor Mrs Weston (poor Miss Taylor that was) would suffer it." (29)

And Frank replies:

"Ah! sir – but a thoughtless young person will sometimes step behind a window-curtain, and throw up a sash without its being suspected. I have often known it done myself."

Frank's teasing here is wonderfully comic. It is also, like the act itself, refreshing. "Frank throws open windows in the novel in a more modern sense," says John Wiltshire: he gives us the chance to judge characters and events "within a different ethic". Through Frank, we have the possibility of "seeing things another way – one that allows much more to impetuosity and surprise, to passion and risk-taking". Mr Woodhouse wants to shut out the world, Frank does not; and the novel here encourages us to see that the world is more volatile than Mr Woodhouse's window-shutting fussiness and Mr Knightley's masculine rationality will allow it to be.

That Emma should be fascinated by Frank Churchill is only natural. He is the outside world incarnate, with hints of Byronic dash about him. She is bored and playful; she does in fact "despise" Highbury and can find it "dull and insipid", and she lives, as an "imaginist", more in the world of ideas than of facts. We are told that "there was something in the name, in the idea of Frank Churchill, which always interested her" (14). In contrast to Mr Knightley, who stands for what Tony Tanner calls "stasis, clarity, traditional routine and a kind of deeply rooted dutifulness", Frank Churchill likes riddles and mysteries and dancing and is an inveterate schemer. So is Emma. To Emma, writes Janet Todd,

> he is not just the prized son of the village but – and here his first name comes into play – a contrast to the very English George Knightley in his stagey French flirtatiousness, his fashionable triviality and ennui, his deceit, restlessness and rootlessness. He is even "sick of England", a statement made just after Emma sees the apotheosis of Englishness at Donwell.

The stage is set for a sustained comedy of misunderstanding. Emma's romantic imagination combines with Frank's deviousness to lead her into sustained and serious error. Frank himself is more than happy to be gallant to Emma, partly as a cover for his secret attachment to Jane but also because he enjoys a light-hearted flirtation – or so we plausibly suppose. Early in their acquaintance he promises: "I will speak the truth, and nothing suits me so well." This may be accurate in a narrow, limited sense, as Frank exploits the ambivalent relationship between language and truth, but he deceives Emma from the beginning and his deceptions are deliberate and artful.

Emma makes his task easy. Not only does she fail to perceive his relationship with Jane Fairfax – convinced, from his remarks about Jane, that he doesn't even like her very much – she conceives the idea that Jane is having an adulterous affair with Mr Dixon, the husband of her protector's daughter, Miss Campbell, and at the party given by the Coleses, persuades herself that Jane's new piano is in fact a present from Mr Dixon. Frank plays along with this, of course, which makes Emma even more confident in her conjectures. At least in her eyes, she and Frank now act out a conspiratorial role, casting themselves as the two in the know, possessed of a shared "intelligence". Once again, Emma's imagination and vanity have misled her – and while she will eventually come to realise that Mr Knightley's assessment of Frank Churchill was more accurate than her own, it will be a long time before she does.

Why does Emma so badly misunderstand both Frank and Jane?

As is often pointed out, Jane Fairfax is much more like a conventional fictional heroine than Emma is. Elegant, pretty and intelligent, Jane is also accomplished; she both sings and plays the piano well. She suffers much during the novel, and her sufferings are exacerbated by Emma. Educated to become a governess, "the very few hundred pounds which she inherited from her father making independence impossible", she has to endure, as Susan Morgan puts it, the "brainless babbling" of her aunt, Miss Bates, Mrs Elton's condescension and Frank's "cruel flirting"*. Towards the end Jane becomes so unhappy she makes herself ill. Having quarrelled with Frank, she "languishes in her cramped room with the intolerably garrulous Miss Bates, having lost her beloved and having nothing to hope for but the terribly crass fate of looking after other people's children..."

*Jane's father, we learn in passing, died in action fighting the French enemy. Frank Churchill has not troubled himself to fight for his country – or do any work of any kind.

Nor is she as virtuous and dull as sometimes seen: in committing herself to Frank she shows herself capable of rash, impulsive behaviour; she is, we may guess from the clues given us and the few words of her own the text allows her, passionate and torn by conflicting feelings.

Yet the girl we see through Emma's eyes is complacent, cold and tiresome. Emma dislikes her, attributing her dislike to Jane's reserve – a reserve explained by her engagement – though it has really originated in jealousy.

Why she did not like Jane Fairfax might be a difficult question to answer; Mr Knightley had once told her it was because she saw in her the really accomplished young woman, which she wanted to be thought herself; and though the accusation had been refuted at the time, there were moments of self-examination in which her conscience could not quite acquit her. (20)

Her imagination wildly misleads her, as Andrew Gibson points out, and in a way "that is indirectly and insidiously self-flattering". By imagining Jane is having an affair with Mr Dixon, Emma simply reinforces her own opinion of Jane's worth. "Her imagination allows her spuriously to exalt herself at Jane's expense." This particular piece of imagining, which she shares with Frank, shows Emma at her worst. Adultery is not a small thing in

"I am very sorry, Miss Fairfax, to hear of your being out this morning in the rain." Mr Woodhouse and Jane Fairfax

the world of Austen's fiction. When Emma first comes up with the "ingenious and animating suspicion" that Jane has been involved illicitly with Dixon, her assumptions are not just false, they are, says Gibson, "extremely demeaning to Jane". Emma imagines Jane to be guilty of thoroughly "mischievous" conduct (20). She imagines Jane, in fact, as "having seduced Mr Dixon's affections from his wife". Emma's fantasy thus serves as grounds for her sense of moral superiority over Jane.

She soon realises this fantasy is wrong-headed, though not because she learns the truth. Her original suspicions have been prompted by Miss

Bates's stories of her niece, but once Emma actually meets Jane the image of her as a temptress dissolves. Struck by Jane's "appearance of ill-health" (20), her attitude changes to one of pity; Jane is in love with Dixon but it is now a hopeless love, "a simple, single, successless love on her side alone, a sad poison". Emma has no more evidence for this view than for the previous one: it is the product, once again, of her romantic imagination. Her initial conception of Jane as immoral, says Gibson,

> was crudely demeaning. It was in fact too crude to satisfy Emma's sophisticated imagination. So she substitutes a more subtly demeaning view of Jane as a terribly pitiable figure, deserving only "compassion and respect". Either way, Emma derives a comforting sense of superiority from her own fantasy. As a respectable woman, she can reflect with "complacency" on Jane's guilt.

The situation, of course, is full of ironies. For one thing, the real secret doesn't involve Emma at all: it is between Frank and Jane. For another, Emma is upset when she learns the truth, condemning Frank and Jane for forming "a league in secret to judge us all" when in fact she, Emma, was more than happy to form a secret "league" of her own with Frank. And Emma's delusions about Jane are in part motivated by her delusions about Frank:

she fancies that she, not Jane, is the object of his love.

In this, she couldn't be more wrong. Her mistake with Frank is the opposite of her mistake with Mr Elton. She thought Mr Elton in love with someone else when he was in love with her; she thinks Frank in love with her when he is in love with someone else.

Her misunderstanding of Frank is profound. To Emma, the gift of the piano to Jane is simply a stimulus for crude speculation. Would Mr Dixon, even if he were involved with a governess, do anything as reckless as give her a piano? Emma has little actual knowledge of how clandestine sex is conducted. In fact, as John Wiltshire has

PIANOS

The piano Frank chooses for Jane, a "square" Broadwood, is valuable and thoughtfully selected. Among the early customers for Broadwood pianos were the wives of Nelson and Wellington; Beethoven, Liszt, Chopin and Mendelsson all played on them.

Several of Austen's heroines play the piano. Emma plays adequately though, we are told, would benefit from practising more. Jane Fairfax's superior playing is a major reason for Emma's jealousy. Jane Austen herself played for an hour every morning before breakfast (which she had at the unfashionably early hour of 9am) ∎

observed, it is a highly romantic present – but the romantic element in Frank and Jane's situation is "simply foreign to [Emma's] sensibility". It becomes clear that the pair fell in love over music, and that music is important to Jane in a way Emma cannot really understand. At the Bates's, the night after the Westons' party, Frank begs Jane to play the piano. What he says is revealing:

> *"If you are very kind... it will be one of the waltzes we danced last night; – let me live them over again... I believe you were glad we danced no longer; but I would have given worlds – all the worlds one ever has to give – for another half hour." (28)*

THE FRENCH CONNECTION

Though *Emma* was first published in December 1815, the novel makes no overt reference to the great political upheavals of the last few decades. More than 20 years of war with France – spanning most of Austen's life up until that point – had culminated on 18th June 1815 with the Battle of Waterloo, less than three months after Austen finished the novel on 29th March. The economic impact of blockades during that conflict had been felt in industry and agriculture for some time. William Baker hails Mr Martin as a "fine example" of the farmers who worked hard to increase crop yield, studying his Agricultural Reports with due care. (*A Critical*

Evidently Frank's gift of the piano is heartfelt, and it is well chosen: a symbol of culture and gentility, it holds the promise for Jane of a more exciting future, one not confined to the Bates's two rooms. When the engagement is broken off, and Jane faces the prospect of becoming a governess, Miss Bates reports her addressing the piano directly: "'You must go,' said she. 'You and I must part. You will have no business here'" (54).

So while Emma is busily constructing a tawdry romantic narrative around Jane, the reader is at the same time being given the material to substantiate a conception of love that is, indeed, romantic – a love that seems to have been more or less at first sight, that is expressed by both in

---

Companion to Jane Austen; A Literary Reference to her Life and Work, 2008).

For all this, the overarching impression of Highbury life is one of stability, at a remove from politics. Over the years, critics have debated whether this picture represents a shallowness of vision in Austen's depiction of society, with varying conclusions. Paula Byrne calls disparagement of Austen's work on such grounds "the silliest of all

criticisms... She wrote about what she understood and no artist can do more." (*Jane Austen's Emma; A Sourcebook,* 2004).

In the character of Frank Churchill, Austen deliberately sets her outsider – charming, vain and lacking in moral fibre – at odds with the ideals of Mr Knightley, the archetypal English gentleman. This is most acutely expressed in Mr Knightley's criticism of Frank to Emma:

passionate terms, and that is carried on in defiance of social proprieties. "Had [Jane] refused" to become engaged, Frank later writes, "I should have gone mad". This intensity – Jane herself, not given to gush, speaks of Frank's "bewitching" qualities – is all the more remarkable because it conflicts with, or is set up in opposition to, the notion of companionate love that is developed through the story of *Emma*. For the novel, which celebrates rational marriage, also offers credence to passionate and reckless love; despite Emma's jaundiced view of Jane, and Mr Knightley's of Frank, the picture we are given of Frank and Jane

No, Emma, your amiable young man can be amiable only in French, not in English…"

Mr Knightley, Roger Sales points out, "displays Francophobia before Frank arrives in Highbury. It is Francophobia in a double sense; dislike of the country as well as jealousy of a man called Frank."

It is not, however, the only moment in which Austen argues for Englishness over European, cosmopolitan values. In Chapter 42, poring over "views of Swisserland", Frank complains that he is "sick of England"; "as soon as my aunt gets well, I shall go abroad". "[His] conversation," Sales notes, "is sprinkled with French words and phrases" and so too are the words that others link to him; words like finessing, manoeuvring and espionage. Frank talks of naïveté and calls Jane's hairstyle outrée.

His character contrasts, not just with that of Highbury's enclosed world, but with Austen's model of Englishness as a whole ∎

is not unsympathetic. Both orphans, without the luxury of money, neither can act with the freedom of Mr Knightley or Emma – hence the need for secrecy. Though Frank behaves badly, he arguably behaves no worse than Emma – her treatment of Harriet is potentially more hurtful than any of Frank's actions; and though Emma and Mr Knightley later discuss the virtues of "openness", Frank and Jane are much quicker to understand their own hearts than Emma or Mr Knightley. And Jane's sufferings in the novel, kept entirely to herself, are far worse than anything Emma has to go through.

This, then, is the real, if largely implicit, background to the relationship between Frank and Emma and the misunderstandings between them. At first he encourages her wrong-headed speculations, but later he changes his mind. Just before leaving Highbury, in an agitated interview, he wants to tell her the truth:

> *"In short," said he, "perhaps, Miss Woodhouse – I think you can hardly be without suspicion" – He looked at her, as if wanting to read her thoughts. She hardly knew what to say. It seemed like the forerunner of something absolutely serious, which she did not wish. (30)*

Ironically, therefore, it is Emma's fault that she doesn't hear the truth from Frank. Because she

TEN FACTS
ABOUT *EMMA*

1.

Austen earned less than £40 from *Emma* during
her lifetime – which would amount to just under
£3,000 today. It was published by the most
respectable of London publishers, John Murray.

2.

One of Jane Austen's admirers was H.R.H. the
Prince Regent. Through the Prince's librarian,
Austen was invited to dedicate one of her works to
the prince. She complied with the royal command
in dedicating *Emma* though her reluctance to do
so is apparent in her wording: "To His Royal
Highness the Prince Regent, this work is, by His
Royal Highness's permission, most respectfully
dedicated, by His Royal Highness's dutiful and
obedient humble servant."

3.

Emma has been the subject of many adaptations. The first film, released in 1948, starred Judy Campbell as Emma. The book was loosely adapted to provide the plot of the 1995 film *Clueless*, starring Alicia Silverstone as Cher Horowitz (Emma). A 1996 production starred Gwyneth Paltrow and in 2010 *Aisha*, a Hindi language version, was released, starring Sonam Kapoor. Other famous Emmas include Kate Beckinsale and Romola Garai.

4.

The only married woman in Austen's novels to call her husband by his Christian name is Mary Musgrove in *Persuasion*. When Mr Knightley asks Emma in Chapter 53 to call him "George" she says: "Impossible! I never can call you any thing but 'Mr Knightley'." And Frank Churchill says in his letter to Mrs Weston explaining his conduct that he hated Mrs Elton calling his fiancée Jane. "'Jane', indeed! – You will observe that I have not yet indulged myself in calling her by that name, even to you."

5.

Emma is the only one of Austen's novels to be titled after its heroine. (Imagine: *Catherine, Elizabeth, Fanny, Anne, Elinor* and *Marianne*.) The name was notorious as being that of Nelson's mistress, Emma Hamilton – a fact of which, as a member of a nautical family, Austen would have been aware. Hamilton died in 1815 – the year in which the novel was published.

6.

Though Austen's work is full of a sense of the precariousness of life, death itself features little. The only two people to die are Dr Grant in *Mansfield Park* and Mrs Churchill in *Emma*.

7.

Two important characters in *Emma* never speak. One is Robert Martin. The other is Mr Perry, the local apothecary, though his words are constantly cited by Mr Woodhouse and others. "Never has a character had so much speech reported by other characters without any of it ever being quoted by the author," notes John Mullan. "The novelist keeps him from speaking, imitating his own canny reticence."

8.

According to her nephew, James Edward Austen-Leigh, Austen " would, if asked, tell us many little particulars about the subsequent career of some of her people". We learn in the case of *Emma*, that "Mr Woodhouse survived his daughter's marriage, and kept her and Mr Knightley from settling at Donwell, about two years; and that the letters placed by Frank Churchill before Jane Fairfax, which she swept away unread, contained the word 'pardon'". We also learn that "the delicate Jane Fairfax lived only another nine or ten years after her marriage to Frank Churchill".

9.

Emma is the only one of Austen's novels in which the heroine doesn't travel at all. The others don't travel much: Elinor and Marianne Dashwood go to London, Elizabeth Bennet goes to Derbyshire; Catherine Morland to Gloucestershire and Northanger; Fanny Price to Portsmouth; and Anne Elliot to Lyme Regis. But Emma never moves from Highbury.

10.

Austen fans were mildly outraged by the casting of Gwyneth Paltrow as Emma in the 1996 Hollywood film. She didn't seem physically robust enough, and her eyes were blue not hazel. Here is Mrs Weston: "Such an eye! The true hazle eye – and so brilliant! regular features, open countenance, with a complexion! oh! what a bloom of full health, and such a pretty height and size; such a firm and upright figure. There is health, not merely in her bloom, but in her air, her head, her glance."

doesn't "wish" to hear something "serious", she stops Frank from going on. She thinks Frank is going to tell her he loves her; in fact he wants to tell her he is betrothed to Jane. If he tells her about Jane it will shatter her illusions and deeply wound her vanity. But if he tells her he loves *her*, Emma, then Emma will have to admit that she doesn't love *him* – and this she doesn't want to do. The "hopes and illusions she imagines him as nursing will be at an end", says Andrew Gibson.

But so will the flattery they offer her, and she wants that flattery to continue. So she cuts him off, and, at the same time, cuts herself off from the truth. The scene is a marvellously ironic account of the mechanisms of a vain imagination at their most intricate.

In balance and contrast to this moment is Emma's exchange with Mr Knightley in Chapter 49, after Emma has recognised the mistakes she has made about Frank and Jane. It is the moment in which Mr Knightley, at last, is trying to declare his love for Emma. Emma, however, wants to stop him just as she stopped Frank. She thinks he is going to declare his love for Harriet:

"Emma, I must tell you what you will not ask, though I may wish it unsaid the next moment." "Oh! then don't speak of it," she eagerly cried.

"Take a little time, consider, do not commit yourself."

"Thank you," said he, in an accent of deep mortification, and not another syllable followed. (49)

As Andrew Gibson observes, this scene "ironically reverses the earlier scene with Frank". In the first scene, Emma imagines a declaration when none is intended; this time she imagines a confession of love for another woman when a declaration to her *is* intended. The scene neatly catches the way she has been humbled, and the self-reproach she feels. By the time of Mr Knightley's confession she is so chastened that she is almost more inclined to believe in Harriet's worth than her own.

How important is Box Hill?

In the second half of the novel, Emma, though still headstrong and blind, gradually begins to show signs of greater self-awareness and her "tenderness of heart", always incipient, begins to manifest itself. She realises she is not in love with Frank Churchill; she meddles less intrusively in Harriet's affairs (while continuing to weave fantasies about her); and for the first time she comes to feel sympathy for Jane Fairfax, beleaguered as she is by the egregious Mrs Elton.

Mrs Elton, handled with a Swiftian

ruthlessness, is one of Austen's great comic creations. Emma, whose first impression is that Mrs Elton has "ease" but not elegance, doesn't take long to judge her character:

the quarter of an hour quite convinced her that Mrs Elton was a vain woman, extremely well satisfied with herself, and thinking much of her own importance; that she meant to shine and be very superior, but with manners which had been formed in a bad school, pert and familiar; that all

GOVERNESSES

The prospect of becoming a governess haunted all middle-class girls unless, like Emma, they were lucky enough to have a fortune of their own. Jane Fairfax dreads life as a governess. "With the fortitude of a devoted novitiate, she had resolved at one-and-twenty to complete the sacrifice and retire from all the pleasures of life, of rational

intercourse, equal society, peace, and hope, to penance and mortification forever" (20). In later conversation with Mrs Elton, she is even more bitter. "There are places in town, offices, where inquiry would produce something – offices for the sale not quite of human flesh, but of human intellect" (35). She is not sure whether governesses, nuns, or slaves are more miserable.

Jane's possible fate makes Emma feel, after everything has come out, that her earlier secrecy about Frank Churchill is almost justified: "If a woman can ever be excused for *her notions were drawn from one set of people, and one style of living; that if not foolish she was ignorant... (32)*

Mrs Elton is like a caricature of Emma: Emma without the good breeding and natural grace. Her imperious determination to "do" for other people and to ride over their wishes; her insufferable vanity; her condescension towards those she considers beneath her – all of this is reminiscent of Austen's complicated heroine at her worst. But

thinking only of herself, it is in a situation like Jane Fairfax's" (46). Though Mrs Weston, as Miss Taylor, has been a governess (to Emma herself), she was lucky, becoming part of the Woodhouse family, and being treated with courtesy by Mr Woodhouse. Jane would almost certainly have fared less well.

The yearly salary for a private governess ranged from £15 to £100 – when Charlotte Bronte worked as one in 1841 her wage was £20 a year (about £1,500 today). Although provided with food and shelter, a governess was expected to buy or make her own clothes and had no security of employment. She was often an isolated figure, cut off from life upstairs but not quite fitting in downstairs either. "I don't like them governesses, Pinner," says the cook in *Vanity Fair* of Becky Sharp. "They give themselves the hairs and hupstarts of ladies, and their wages is no better than you nor me." Becky and Jane Eyre are the two most famous governesses in 19th-century literature; the last to appear is in Henry James's ghost story, *The Turn of the Screw*, which is narrated by a governess ∎

while Emma herself may not see the parallels, she is quick enough to perceive Mrs Elton's faults – a reminder that, unlike Mrs Elton, she is clever and capable of making sensible judgements. Seeing Emma alongside Mrs Elton only makes us more aware of Emma's good qualities.

But, Emma's bad behaviour is not yet over, and her worst, most famous, lapse, comes at the ill-fated party at Box Hill, a party marred by listlessness and general bad feeling at which no one enjoys themselves and everyone splits into small groups – a party which, John Bayley shrewdly points out, has some similarity with the amateur theatricals in *Mansfield Park* "in its revelation of the *too much* tried for, the overacted social effort". Emma's forced merriment stems from disappointment: still ignorant of Frank's attachment to Jane, she flirts outrageously with him not from any "real felicity" but rather "because she felt less happy than she had expected". She is then gratuitously rude to Miss Bates.

The searing rebuke Mr Knightley delivers to Emma the day after this makes all too plain the difference between him and Frank. "The difference between his friendship, with its unsparing stress on facts, however unpleasant, and the trivial flattery of Frank Churchill, could not be made more clear," says Frank Bradbrook. "There are few more effective denunciations of heartlessness than this short speech by a character who personifies everything that Jane Austen most respects."

Mr Knightley begins by saying he "must once more speak to her":

"I cannot see you acting wrong, without a remonstrance. How could you be so unfeeling to Miss Bates? How you could you be so insolent to a woman of her character, age and situation? – Emma, I had not thought it possible." (43)

As well as insolence, he charges her with insensitivity and the irresponsible use of her cleverness against an innocent victim; she has talked to Miss Bates as if she did not count. A bore Miss Bates may be, but her age, poverty and dependence should draw Emma's compassion, as Mr Knightley insists, not her contempt. The narrator has been careful to make this point when introducing Miss Bates in the novel's third chapter:

Miss Bates, neither young, handsome, rich, nor married, stood in the very worst predicament in the world for having much of the public favour; and she had no intellectual superiority to make atonement to herself, or frighten those who might hate her, into outward respect. (3)

As the distinguished Austen scholar Marilyn Butler has pointed out, Box Hill is a moral nadir for Frank as well as for Emma. By flirting with

Emma he inflicts intolerable pain on the girl he really loves. Emma may be less guilty in relation to Jane, because, though she sees afterwards that she must have "stabbed Jane Fairfax's peace in a thousand instances", she is not aware of it at the time. Yet, as Butler reminds us, Emma *does* believe Harriet to be in love with the man with whom she is flirting, and the hurt to Miss Bates "is not therefore a single instance, for there is a pattern in the novel of vulnerable single women, whom it is the social duty of the strong and rich to protect".

This time, however, Mr Knightley's words strike home. Emma, finally, is deeply touched.

> *Never had she felt so agitated, mortified, grieved, at any circumstance in her life... The truth of his representation there was no denying. She felt it in her heart. How could she have been so brutal, so cruel to Miss Bates? (43)*

From now she begins to act with true tenderness of heart. She goes to see Miss Bates the next day, determined to make amends; she tries harder than ever – though for a long time unsuccessfully – to make amends to Jane; she is kinder than ever to her father. Along the way come two shocks which make her further doubt her own judgment. The first is the news of the betrothal of Frank to Jane; secondly, she finds that the "very superior person" with whom Harriet is in love is not Frank but Mr Knightley. Together, these shocks shake the foundations of her world, built as it has been on blindness, vanity and fantasy. At long last she realises that "Mr Knightley must marry no one but herself". She looks deeply into her own heart and is miserable:

To understand, thoroughly understand, her own heart was the first endeavour. To that point went every leisure moment which her father's claims on her allowed... (47)

At the end of the novel, Frank feels free to joke about his blunder – publicly mentioning the rumour about Mr Perry buying a new carriage which he could only have learnt from Jane. Emma laughs with him or at least smiles "completely". But this is only "for a moment". She sees, now, that Frank has caused Jane more heartache than he needed to, especially at Box Hill, and she sees why: he didn't just deceive his elders, he *enjoyed* doing it. He indulged himself in fantasy. But Emma knows herself better now. She is seeing with Mr Knightley's eyes, and "felt, that pleased as she had been to see Frank Churchill and really regarding him as she did with friendship, she had never been more sensible of Mr Knightley's high superiority of character" (54). When Mrs Weston asks her to postpone judgement of Frank until his letter of explanation arrives, she won't wait and her response is immediate:

> *"It has sunk him, I cannot say how it has sunk him in my opinion. So unlike what a man should be! – None of that upright integrity, that strict adherence to truth and principle, that disdain of trick and littleness, which a man should display in every transaction of his life." (46)*

One must be careful not to overstate the change in Emma. Austen's heroines develop but are never transformed, and Emma – always doing "more than she wished and less than she ought" – remains Emma. She is deeply unsettled as she looks back at her treatment of the Martins, of Harriet, of Jane Fairfax and Miss Bates, but, as Julia Prewitt Brown wisely notes, "her disposition is to like and accept herself wholeheartedly" – which is one of the reasons we like her.

How blind is Mr Knightley?

Mr Knightley was said to be Jane Austen's favourite portrait of a traditional country gentleman. He is thoughtful and kind to his "inferiors"; unlike Mrs Elton's vulgar attentions to Jane, and Emma's self-gratifying patronage of Harriet, his attempts to help others are delicate,

"Oh, Mr Knightley, one moment more." Miss Bates and Mr Knightley

discreet and unselfish, whether he is giving his last apples to Miss Bates, asking Harriet to dance after she has been snubbed, assisting Robert Martin, or behaving tactfully and patiently with Mr Woodhouse.

He makes his first appearance at Hartfield with appropriate quietness: "a visitor... walked in". As Janet Todd observes, his initial remarks are cool and he appears more like a brother or substitute father than a future lover, but there is an interesting sprightliness in his exchange with Emma about match-making. Mr Knightley disparages Emma's claims to have brought Mr Weston and Miss Taylor together as merely a "lucky guess"; she responds by teasing him: "And you have never known the pleasure and triumph of a lucky guess? – I pity you. – I thought you cleverer" (1). The exchange, says Todd, "has something of the impudent flirtation of Elizabeth and Darcy [in *Pride and Prejudice*] but is more barbed, more embedded in familial habit".

Despite the 17-year age difference, the relationship between Emma and Mr Knightley is essentially a relationship of equals, says John Wiltshire, and the verbal contests between them reflect this. When they fight over Harriet Smith and Robert Martin, Emma may be in the wrong, but underlying the real anger on both sides, "there is a reciprocation of energy, a love of the other's strength of mind". She enjoys crossing swords with him; he draws out her wit and fire; he stimulates her ingenuity. "You are very fond of bending little minds; but when little minds belong to rich people in authority, I think they have a knack of swelling out, till they are quite as unmanageable as great ones," she says at one point (18). Like so much of what she says, this has the ring of intuitive truth.

There is an erotic content in their exchanges from the beginning, but it is implicit: this is a story of two people who love each other but are unaware of the fact. Mr Knightley later says to Emma that he has been "in love with you ever since you were thirteen at least" (52), but he only realises this in retrospect. As John Mullan says, Emma's brief absences from the novel are used to show "the true folly of her schemes" – we see Mr Knightley guessing the truth about Frank Churchill and Jane Fairfax, so its revelation will not be as much a surprise to us as it is to Emma. But the absences are also used to show Mr Knightley's own delusions. When Emma is first absent, in Chapter Five, he says to Mrs Weston:

"I should like to see Emma in love, and in some doubt of a return; it would do her good. But there is nobody hereabouts to attach her..."

Mrs Weston listens but conceals her own thoughts – at this stage she and Mr Weston appear to have Frank Churchill in mind as a husband for

Emma. Meanwhile Mr Knightley's "nobody heareabouts", says Mullan, only draws attention to "his own obtuseness about his deeper feelings for Emma". He is similarly obtuse when Mrs Weston praises Emma's beauty and he replies:

> *"I confess that I have seldom seen a face or figure more pleasing to me than her's. But I am a partial old friend."*

Looks and physical presence are hugely important in Austen, as Mullan says, and here Mr Knightley is "sizing up [Emma's] body as well as appreciating her features" and doing so "with something more than the language of an 'old friend'". But he is entirely unconscious of it. Only a shock, or series of shocks, it seems, will jolt him and Emma out of their mutual blindness.

One problem is the gap in years between them. Peter Hollindale has shown how important age is in the novel: in many cases it is very precisely given. Emma herself is nearly 21, we learn in the first sentence; Mr Knightley is "a sensible man about seven or eight-and-thirty"; Mr Elton "six or seven-and-twenty"; Robert Martin 24: "*Only* four-and-twenty", according to Emma, a problem of inconvenient youthfulness which Mr Elton at six-and-twenty has presumably overcome. Harriet is 17, Frank is 23, and Isabella, Emma's sister, is seven years older than she is. Yet for all the emphasis on actual age, the novel suggests, says Hollindale, that true age "must be computed by something more than the number of birthdays passed".

An example of this comes early, when we are told that Mr Woodhouse (one of the few characters whose exact age is not given) has been "a valetudinarian all his life" and is "a much older man in ways than in years". Though friendly and amiable, "his talents could not have recommended him at any time" (1).

That age is important in the relationship between Emma and Mr Knightley becomes clearer when they argue in Chapter 12. Mr Knightley warns Emma about behaving too much "under the power of fancy"; to which she smartly retorts: "To be sure – our discordancies must always arise from my being in the wrong." He says, smiling: "Yes... and reason good. I was sixteen years old when you were born." Emma acknowledges that he was undoubtedly much her superior at that period of their lives:

"...but does not the lapse of one-and-twenty years bring our understandings a good deal nearer?"

"Yes – a good deal nearer."

"But still not near enough to give me a chance of being right, if we think differently."

"I still have the advantage of you by sixteen years' experience, and by not being a pretty young

woman and a spoiled child. Come, my dear Emma, let us be friends and say no more about it." (12)

This is a revealing exchange, with Emma giving as good as she gets. Mr Knightley's description of her as "a pretty young woman and a spoiled child" shows it is not just Emma who has much to learn. He manages to be both provocatively condescending ("spoiled child") and flattering ("pretty young woman") at the same time. In fact, Emma is right: the gap between their ages is closing, and fast, though it will require the arrival of the 23-year-old Frank Churchill to wake Mr Knightley up. Through bitter experience, says Hollindale, Emma grows older. "What is less obvious is that Mr Knightley grows younger."

At first he strikes us as somewhat limited. He can be socially awkward – he is unnecessarily brusque about Emma's portrait of Harriet – and on occasions even downright rude, reminding us of his bad-tempered brother. Although he is right about Emma's behaviour at Box Hill, he has earlier snapped at Miss Bates himself about allowing Jane to sing too much: "Are you mad?" – and later he talks loudly over her. And he refuses to dance, something, as Janet Todd points out, which "damns Mr Darcy [in *Pride and Prejudice*] in a gathering of supernumerary ladies". Emma watches him at the Westons' party.

She was more disturbed by Mr Knightley's not dancing than by anything else. There he was, among the standers-by, where he ought not to be; he ought to be dancing – not classing himself with the husbands and fathers and whist players. (38)

But if he initially seems emotionally retarded,

MR KNIGHTLEY'S SEX LIFE

The inevitable question arises: is Mr Knightley – now middle-aged – "pure"? Has he kept himself virginal, like some Sir Galahad, for Emma? Deirdre le Faye speculates: "It is not excessively far-fetched (if somewhat un-Austenish) to suspect that Mr Knightley has a respectable lower-class mistress tucked away somewhere; not, obviously, in Donwell, to offend the neighbours, but maybe some innkeeper's wife/widow or similar, whom he visits when he goes to Richmond or Kingston markets."

Similarly hard-nosed critics may speculate that Mr Knightley has waited all these years because he has his eye not just on Emma but on her £30,000. Mr Knightley's farming interests are not going wonderfully well – "improvement" is proving expensive. The upkeep of Donwell Abbey has become expensive. Mr Knightley's brother, John, has contrived to make himself a successful London lawyer with Woodhouse money. That money may well have also added lustre to Emma's juvenile charms. ∎

when he later rescues Harriet from her snub by Mr Elton and begins to dance with her – and, to Emma's surprise, dance *well* – he suddenly seems both more mature *and* younger. Emma observes this immediately. She registers his "tall, firm, upright figure"; after dinner, her "eyes invited him irresistibly to come to her and be thanked"; he looks at her with "smiling penetration" and they banter about Mr Elton before dancing together. It is a romantic scene, conveyed with brilliant economy, the kind of scene, Virginia Woolf argues, which the author of *Middlemarch* could never have achieved. The trouble with George Eliot, says Woolf, is that her "hold upon dialogue... is slack":

> She allows her heroines to talk too much. She has little verbal felicity. She lacks the unerring taste which chooses one sentence and compresses the heart of the scene into that. "Whom are you going to dance with?" asked Mr Knightley, at the Westons' ball. "With you, if you will ask me," said Emma; and she has said enough. Mrs Casaubon [the heroine of *Middlemarch*] would have talked for an hour and we should have looked out of the window."

The love which Emma and Mr Knightley feel for one another, says Janet Todd, is not the "hungry, repressed sort" of Fanny Price in *Mansfield Park* or Mr Darcy in *Pride and Prejudice*, but "something more mutual and unexpected". It shows itself in all kinds of quiet ways. When Emma and Harriet discuss a conversation about spruce beer, Emma remembers exactly where Mr Knightley was standing; Mr Knightley, on another occasion, looks sourly at Frank Churchill when he flirts with Emma. But the crucial moment, perhaps, is the visit to Donwell Abbey; upon her arrival Emma soon leaves Mr Knightley in order to

> *look around her; eager to refresh and correct her memory with more particular observation, more exact understanding of a house and grounds which must be ever so interesting to her and all her family. (42)*

The word order is important here, as is that oddly jarring word "must". She puts herself before "all her family". A little later, she takes another opportunity to walk into the hall "for a few moments' free observation of the entrance and ground-plot of the house". As Paul Pickrel says, this seems excessive for someone wondering whether her little nephew may live there a generation hence: "More likely she is considering just what the rooms would look like with new curtains."

Like much of *Emma*, this is a reworking of *Pride and Prejudice*. Elizabeth's trip to Pemberley changes her view of Darcy; she later tells her sister, with a touch of irony perhaps, that she dates her love of him to her first sight of the house and grounds. Donwell is less idealised, less reflective of social power and wealth, but like Pemberley it reflects its owner. "It was just what it ought to be," Emma reflects, "and it looked what it was." It is without fashionable smoothness, says John Wiltshire, "and thus presents or incarnates the blunt honesty, the moral integrity, even what Austen presents as the characteristic Englishness, of its owner".

Emma's desire is represented in the image of Donwell; it is a "resting place" for her dreams where, as Wiltshire puts it, "erotic longing is united with a conservative political and social agenda". It offers permanence, stability and abundance. But while Donwell is sheltered, an outdoor scene in which freedom for Emma is imaginable in an ordered, established world, Box Hill, which immediately follows, offers a different kind of outdoors: an empty space in which people wander off in all directions, social relations are unstructured and what appears to be freedom is really anything but.

Box Hill is the scene of Emma's most painful humiliation – and for the first time in the narrative she shows genuine emotion, crying with shame; later, when Mr Knightley finds she has visited Miss Bates to make amends, he replies with a "glow". What Janet Todd calls "an erotic charge surges from the pain" and the pair move so close to one another that physical boundaries disappear; the moment is captured in the fractured syntax Austen will later fully develop to express deep emotion in *Persuasion*:

> *"He took her hand; – whether she had not herself made the first motion, she could not say – she might, perhaps, have rather offered it – but he took her hand." (45)*

After this, the fear that Mr Knightley is pursuing Harriet slightly unhinges Emma: she can't keep still, starting, sighing and walking about, echoing "unawares the moving misery of Jane Fairfax when her engagement was broken", says Todd. Her body and her mind "unite to feel the arrow of desire". When Mr Knightley proposes to her, the narrator does not give us her response, merely telling us: "What did she say? – Just what she ought, of course. A lady always does" (49). Some have criticised the coyness of this – "What does a lady say? Did Jane Austen actually know? Certainly we'll never know," complains Valentine Cunningham – but the formula reflects the view which emerges from the book (a view also reflected in the brevity of the exchange on the dance floor) that language is of limited value and that words are unsuited to deep emotion. "If I loved you less, I might be able to talk about it more," says Mr

Knightley. It is a highly charged scene: two intelligent people who love each other come together at last, each fearing the other is devoted to someone else, each trying to hold back emotion, each concerned to further the happiness of the other.

It is a scene where looks take over.

> *He stopped in his earnestness to look the question, and the expression of his eyes overpowered her. (49)*

To "look the question" is an extraordinary grammatical usage, observes John Mullan. "As if only looking can express meaning"; looking in Austen "is perhaps never more charged with meaning" than it is here.

At this point Emma's love for Mr Knightley becomes her "fever", and the assurance of it gives her a "sleepless" night. Motherhood, which she once rejected, forms "part of her erotic vision", says Todd, and as she remembers her earlier supposed concern for the rights of her nephew as heir of Donwell, she gives herself "a saucy conscious smile".

It is astonishing that Emma should have come so far in a few short months. But Austen contrives to make this emotional journey logical and convincing. The way the novel ends is satisfying because it is right: it is not super-imposed, a mere tying up of knots; as a denouement it is both surprising and unsurprising: surprising because of the speed with which it finally happens, unsurprising because it has been so carefully prepared for. As in a good detective novel, there has been a false trail – the possibility of Emma falling for Frank Churchill – but the outcome makes perfect sense; there have been clues throughout which show us as much; because of Austen's wonderfully flexible and ambiguous use of free indirect speech, Emma's love for Mr Knightley is implicit in the story from the beginning. "We all have a better guide in ourselves, if we would attend to it," says Fanny Price in *Mansfield Park*. Emma finally attends to her inner guide – and if we have attended to the clues in the novel we will have realised that her real interest has always been Mr Knightley.

At the end of the novel she is exulting in her good fortune. Her playful pledge never to call her husband George – "I never can call you any thing but 'Mr Knightley'," she insists – is part of this. Only once has she ever called him George, she says, and that was to annoy him. Her determination to keep on calling him Mr Knightley is, perhaps, a sign of her joy. What we call people matters; Emma is desperately happy and wants to freeze the moment; she is resolved not to forget the humbleness she feels, not to let this happy time degenerate into something more frivolous and less special. Love is something we have no right to; Emma, who knows this, is grateful and relieved to have found it. Suddenly Mr Knightley is very *un*familiar as well as very familiar – familiar as an old friend, unfamiliar in his new role as lover, and Emma's self-conscious determination to go on calling him Mr Knightley is a game she plays with herself – a way of hugging to herself the new realisation of her feeling for him. It echoes Millamant's attitude in Act Four of William Congreve's Restoration Comedy, *The Way of the World*. As the lovers begin premarital negotiations, Millamant says: "I won't be called names after I'm married; positively I won't be called names."

MIRABELL: Names!
MILLAMANT: Aye, as wife, spouse, my dear, joy, jewel, love, sweetheart, and the rest of the nauseous cant, in which men and their wives are so fulsomely familiar – I shall never bear that!

Like Millamant, Emma is determined not to knuckle under and dwindle into being merely a wife. Her insistence on going on saying "Mr Knightley" has been seen as a sign of submissiveness but it is much more complicated than that.

Mr Knightley, for his part, seems altogether

"He stopped in his earnestness to look the question, and the expression of his eyes overpowered her." Mr Knightley declares his love for Emma.

younger than he did, with Austen, as Hollindale says, having some fun at his expense. His "plunge into romantic youthfulness" is "comically testified" by Mr Elton, who, after enduring a hot walk to Donwell to meet him, finds Mr Knightley has uncharacteristically forgotten the arrangement and wandered off: "Perhaps to Hartfield, perhaps to the Abbey Mill, perhaps into his woods" (52).

He also shows "comic instability" of judgement during his courtship, veering from harbouring a still deeper hostility towards Frank Churchill to forgiving him completely.

He had found her agitated and low. – Frank Churchill was a villain. – He heard her declare that she had never loved him. Frank Churchill's character was not desperate. – She was his own Emma, by hand and word, when they returned into the house; and if he could have thought of Frank Churchill then, he might have deemed him a very good fellow. (49)

For all his long acquaintance with her Mr Knightley has repeatedly misconstrued Emma, as she on her side has misconstrued him; after getting to know Harriet, for example, he praises her for helping to instil good principles in her, a compliment which Emma acknowledges to be "a little more praise than she deserved". As the feminist critic Claudia Johnson observes:

"Harriet was soon assailed."

Knightley is not nearly so wise and all-seeing as he appears to think. He extols "the beauty of truth and sincerity in all our dealings with each other", but many things – fortunately – have escaped his monitorship, Emma's worst faults among them. Knightley never learns, for example, that Emma did not stop with Mr Elton, but proceeded to match Harriet and Frank; nor does he learn that Harriet, for her part, learned enough about gentility to disdain the very idea, and to prefer him instead, which is, after all, more than Emma had the wisdom to do.

Emma, of course, must keep these humiliating little secrets to herself, which means there is a discrepancy between Mr Knightley's knowledge of her and ours; we know more of his intended bride than he does himself. But then knowledge of others, Austen insists, is always partial. As the narrator puts it: "Seldom, very seldom, does complete truth belong to any human disclosure" (49).

What is the significance of all the puzzles, mysteries and word games in *Emma*?

Emma's world is full of games and riddles. In the first chapter, she is about to play backgammon with her father, to get him "tolerably through the evening", when Mr Knightley arrives. The "whist-club night" for gentlemen at the Crown Inn is an important social occasion in Highbury, and Mr Perry is cross when Mr Elton, the best player, absents himself to take Harriet's portrait to London. Mrs Goddard is engaged to play piquet with Mr Woodhouse on the night of the Coles's party. Even at the Martins' farm, games are very important: Harriet tells Emma of their "merry evening games" (4).

That games matter in Highbury is scarcely

surprising: it is a small provincial town where not much happens. Games pass the time. Other pastimes, like hunting, seem to be entirely absent. There is no news other than local gossip; newspapers are never mentioned, even though momentous things are happening in London – during the Regency – and the world at large, wracked as it is by war. Apart from some pilfering of poultry coops – probably those gypsies again – excitement in Highbury is rare, one reason why Emma accepts the invitation to the Coles's party, the alternative being to stay at home "in solitary grandeur" (25).

Suzie Campbell sees a social significance in the games: based as they are on strict rules and regulations, they mirror the rules and regulations of a very structured world which can only function by maintaining, as she puts it, "a very particular order". Marriages, friendships and indeed all social intercourse are governed by these rules. At the ball at the Crown Inn, "Mr Weston and Mrs Elton led the way, Mr Frank Churchill and Miss Woodhouse followed. Emma must submit to stand second to Mrs Elton..." (38). On the ill-fated Box Hill trip, Mrs Elton asserts her superior status as a married woman. "Everyone knows what is due to you," says her husband. Emma is put out by Frank Churchill's casual attitude to social hierarchies, thinking that "his indifference to a confusion of rank, bordered too much on inelegance of mind"(24).

The most important games in *Emma* are word-games, which are central to a novel itself so concerned with the problems and limitations of language: they reflect the difficulties the characters have understanding one another. Amidst the mysteries and puzzles of the novel, from the origins of Jane's piano to the central secret of her engagement to Frank, are a series of these games.

Emma is as accomplished a misreader of riddles as she is of letters. Her attempts to decipher letters, as we have seen, begin with her closed-minded misreading of Robert Martin's strong, unaffected

THE NATURAL WORLD IN *EMMA*

Emma is often noted for the vividness of its country setting. Austen's brother Frank declared that he "liked it better than either [*Pride and Prejudice* or *Mansfield Park*] on account of the peculiar air of nature throughout". Walter Scott, writing an unsigned criticism in the *Quarterly Review* of March 1816, agreed; marking a distinction between Austen's work and "the former rules of the novel", full of high incident and far-flown landscapes, he placed *Emma* at the forefront of a new style, "the art of copying from nature as she really exists in the common walks of life". Austen's depiction of the countryside is in line with her view of the rural community, as both full of incident and devoid of artifice. Landscape, and even nature has been proposal of marriage to Harriet, and continue with her finding Frank Churchill's letter to Mrs Weston "stimulative" in Chapter 31 – stimulative because she thinks the references in it to "Miss Woodhouse" are a confirmation that he loves her. Valentine Cunningham notes that "her epistolary errors and mismanagements are central to the comic exposure of 'one who sets up as I do for Understanding' as an egregious misreader of self and world". Nor does Emma understand why Jane is constantly visiting the post office or why she hangs on in Highbury when she might be with her guardians, the Campbells, in Ireland (although no

allowed to take its course, bearing in itself social and economic implications.

When admiring the view of the Martins' farm, Emma allows herself to observe that it has "all the appendages of prosperity and beauty" (42); the one valued in conjunction with the other, and set apart from her own, more snobbish views of the residents within. Meanwhile, Donwell Abbey has "abundance of timber in rows and avenues, which neither fashion nor extravagance had rooted up" – a reflection on Mr Knightley's good taste, unfettered by whim, as well as the long-standing regard in which the Abbey owners have been held. "Indeed," as Rodney Farnsworth observes, "the gardens, orchards, fields and fishponds of Donwell come in for some of the most extensive and elaborate bit of landscape word-painting to be found in the works of Jane Austen; it might further be observed that the picturesque charm of Box Hill is sorely neglected by comparison." (*Mediating Order and Chaos: The* one else solves the mystery either). Jane is a "riddle, quite a riddle", she says at one point. "Here is quite a puzzle" (33).

There are three occasions on which actual riddles or word-puzzles occur in *Emma*. On the first, in Chapter Nine, Emma is the first to catch the *meaning* of Mr Elton's riddle – the answer is "courtship" – but utterly misunderstands its intentions, training them on Harriet. "I cannot have a moment's doubt... You are his object." Emma is similarly blind during the alphabet game in Chapter 41 when Frank Churchill uses the game

---

Water-Cycle in the Complex Adaptive Systems of Romantic Culture). We hear so much about Donwell because it is so much the centre of Emma's developing interest; its nature rings in concordance with her views of what cultivation should be.

Box Hill, by direct contrast – it comes immediately after Emma's time gazing down at Donwell – is characterised by "deficiency" all round; a "want of spirits", and a want of even the shortest descriptive passage to give the beauty spot its due.

Emma is withdrawn, wrapped up in her own feelings of dejection and humiliation; not even the most princely of views could have roused her. But, though almost without outstanding feature in the novel, Austen's setting would have had certain associations among her contemporary readers, as a place with "a more dubious reputation" (Alistair M. Duckworth, annotation to *Emma*, 2002). As early as 1709 it was viewed, as John Mackay wrote in *Tour* at that time, as somewhere where young lovers were able

to send a message to Jane, spelling out the word "blunder", the word "Dixon" and possibly also a third, which remains unspecified. What does it all signify? What is Churchill's game?

The critic John Mullan points out that the word "blunder" is like "a guide to the plot" in *Emma*. It is used 15 times in all; this is "a novel of blunders, of motives misunderstood and secret attachments almost betrayed..." So it is natural and appropriate that 'blunder' should be the word "at the heart of the game that is itself at the heart of the novel". (Austen loved blunders, says Mullan, because they

"insensitively to lose their company in these pretty labyrinths of Box-Wood, and divert themselves unperceived" (ibid., citing J. E. Rogers Jr., "Emma Woodhouse: Betrayed by Place", Persuasions 21, 1999). Emma, thanks to her own indiscretion with Frank Churchill and her grave offence to Miss Bates, finds herself in a different kind of labyrinth; one that threatens to cut her off from all prospects of happiness. Lost as she still is, the full extent of her feelings for Mr Knightley (as the source of that happiness) goes unheeded.

Only on the day when Mr Knightley confesses his feelings for her does Emma look once again at her surroundings with an eye for natural beauty. She sets out on the walk that will lead to that crucial encounter glorying in the "exquisite sight, smell, sensation of nature, tranquil, warm and brilliant after a storm". And when she returns, confident of his affections, she is able to reflect "how often had her eyes fallen on the same shrubs in the lawn, and observed the same beautiful effect of the western sun" (50) ■

"show the difference between what we can understand of her characters, and what they can understand of each other".)

Mr Knightley, the best reader of puzzles in the novel and, unusually, the focal character for this chapter, hits on the truth of this silly anagram. He sees a message is being sent from Frank to Jane. "It was a child's play, chosen to conceal a deeper game on Frank Churchill's part." He sees why Frank has used the word "blunder" and realises why letters have been travelling through the mail between the covert lovers. Emma, once again, sets herself up as a confident reader, but once again is deceived. "My dear Emma," says Mr Knightley, "do you perfectly understand the degree of acquaintance between the gentleman and lady we have been speaking of?" "Oh! yes, perfectly," says Emma, but she doesn't understand it at all, insisting that there "is no admiration between them" (41).

But not even Mr Knightley is able to identify the meaning of "another collection of letters" (making up a third word) which is "anxiously" pushed towards Jane but which is "resolutely swept away by her unexamined". On this confusion, the text is silent. "In other words," says Valentine Cunningham, "the novel's insistence upon the enigmatic difficulties of reading is absorbingly strengthened at this point."

The final game in *Emma* is the gruesome one on Box Hill in which everyone is invited to say one clever thing, two moderately clever things or three dull ones. Emma's truly terrible mistake with Miss Bates is not alleviated by Mr Weston instantly trying to be clever by offering a conundrum. "What two letters of the alphabet are there, that express perfection?" He doesn't wait for an answer, rushing on with his own: "M and A. – Em-ma..." Nothing could be more inappropriate. Frank and Harriet laugh, predictably, given his shallowness and her stupidity, but so, to her shame, does Emma. Mr Knightley is grave. "*Perfection*," he says, "should not have come quite so soon" (43).

The word-games in *Emma* are a reminder of how words can be used to confuse and conceal as well as to enlighten. More clearly than in Austen's other novels, says Janet Todd, language itself is seen as a game.

The point is mirrored in the playfulness of the narrative, and the narrator's language, which simply deceive the first-time reader. Within the story, charades are clearly treacherous but all words have similarly slippery potential, and riddling is only an extreme version of the entire book and much of its dialogue.

Interpretation is never easy, whether of riddles, puzzles, letters or any form of discourse. This is especially true when there are characters like

Frank Churchill to contend with, who delight in fooling others, especially their elders. "What perturbs this novel," says Valentine Cunningham, "is precisely the lack of openness in Emma's world, and it's a lack provocatively embodied, it turns out, in the bearer of a name that's utterly central to the vocabulary of sincerity: one Frank."

What view of the world does *Emma* leave us with?

In *Emma*, "Jane Austen contrives an idyllic world, or the closest approximation to it that the genre of the novel will permit", writes Lionel Trilling. He goes on to say that in the world of Highbury "there are no bad people, and no adverse judgements to be made". It's an odd view, with little support from the text. *Emma* may stand alone in Austen's novels in having no "bad people", but it is full of "adverse judgements" – whether of the odious Eltons, of the people who disparage Miss Bates, or of Frank Churchill, of discourteous John Knightley and even of selfish egotists, like Mr Woodhouse; nor is Emma's egregiously bad behaviour condoned.

There are moments when the novel does offer a vision that is pastoral and very English. When visiting Donwell, Emma looks out over the grounds:

It was a sweet view – sweet to the eye and the

mind. English verdure, English culture, English comfort, seen under a sun bright, without being oppressive. (42)

This view is surely Emma's rather more than the narrator's. (Ironically, it takes in Abbey-Mill Farm, home of the Martins, the place Emma once thought would degrade Harriet but is now quite unconcerned about.) And to Emma it is an idyllic view. In his notes on the novel, R.W. Chapman has pointed out that the reference to the orchard being "in blossom" when the season is "about Midsummer" is "one of Miss Austen's rare mistakes". John Wiltshire excuses the "mistake" on the grounds that Austen is trying to present a fantasy of a pastoral paradise, and one that includes everything: ripe strawberries, sunshine, "spreading flocks", "ample gardens washed by a stream", farmland and a domestic hearth, a picture to satisfy all Emma's desires.*

But this scene of a pastoral idyll is not typical of the book. Lionel Trilling suggests that there is less awareness of economic pressures in *Emma* than there is in Austen's other novels (with the exception of *Northanger Abbey*). It is true that, alone among Austen's heroines, Emma is financially secure. Her problem is that she has

*Meteorologically inclined critics have, however, discovered that the year in which Austen was writing was unseasonally cold, and spring was late in arriving.

too much: rich, spoilt and bored, she is isolated at Hartfield with her father and no financial incentive to marry.

Financial concerns in *Emma* surface or are implied in all sorts of different ways. Mr Elton is too prudent to marry Harriet: he "knows the value of a good income as well as anybody" (8), Mr Knightley tells Emma. We are often reminded of the poverty in Highbury, not least through quiet emphasis on Emma's efforts to help the poor – "[they] were as sure of relief from her personal attention and kindness, her counsel and her patience, as from her purse" (10). Jane's destiny

MARRIAGE

Emma is framed by marriage. It begins with one wedding – that of "poor Miss Taylor" – and ends with three more. In the middle Augusta Hawkins becomes the bride of Mr Elton. The financial aspect of marriage is frequently touched on. We are told that Mr Weston, having "made his fortune", is now at liberty to seek happiness with a "well-judging and truly amiable woman". He is well enough off to marry "a woman as portionless as Miss Taylor". A portion, or dowry, was the money a bride brought to her marriage, which then became her husband's property. Jane Fairfax also has no portion or dowry; Frank can only marry her once his capricious aunt has died. Miss Hawkins brings a dowry of £10,000 to Mr Elton when she marries him; Robert Martin, an up-and-coming farmer, has enough money to look could easily have been to disappear into a kind of limbo as a governess, possibly to a friend of Mrs Elton's, a fate imagined by Austen with grim and vivid realism. Miss Bates's poverty is at the heart of Mr Knightley's rebuke to Emma after Box Hill.

As for Mr Knightley himself: he has a large and valuable estate but, we are told, "little spare money". He struggles to send the Bateses a bushel of apples or get out his carriage to take them to the ball. He works hard, having taken the running of the main farm on his estate into his own hands, and seems to have no steward or assistant except William Larkins. Paul Pickrel speculates that Mr

---

after Harriet.

Austen was well aware that the alternatives to marriage for most middle-class women were bleak. They were doomed to be old maids (like Miss Bates) and if poor to undertake a life of drudgery (as Jane nearly does as a governess). Yet marriage offered little freedom: in effect, wives became the property of their husbands. According to a prominent lawyer in 1758, "the very being or legal existence of a woman is suspended during the marriage or at least is incorporated and consolidated into that of the husband..." It was not until the Married Woman's Property Act of 1882 that women gained any real measure of control over their lives. In *Emma*, both Isabella Knightley and Mrs Weston become totally submissive to their husbands. In practice, many marriages were more equal, as we know Emma's will be: her early renunciation of marriage is understandable in financial terms; in her case, though, it is also a sign of how little she understands herself and the real sources of human happiness ∎

Knightley's father may have left the estate in debt. True or not, his marriage evidently makes economic as well as romantic sense. Mr Knightley's ancestral acres are matched with Emma's ready cash. As well as adding a little frivolity to his life, Emma will be able to make his grounds prettier and enable him to keep the Bateses well stocked with apples. Surely, says Paul Pickrel, "the names Knightley and Donwell Abbey with their suggestion of aristocracy and antiquity combine with the plebeian Woodhouse and the pleasant but unhistorical Hartfield to underline in a quiet way the kind of bridge the marriage makes".

Allied to money in the novel is the ever-present question of class. If *Emma* is a pastoral idyll, it is one frequently undercut by Austen's bitingly subversive irony. We are told early on, for example, that when Miss Churchill married Mr Weston, the marriage took place "to the infinite mortification of Mr and Mrs Churchill, who threw her off with due decorum".

"Due decorum? Who is speaking here?" wonders Tony Tanner. But this is surely an unpleasant parody of "due decorum". Emma herself later reflects on the arbitrariness and injustice of social designations which can produce this heartless rejection of a daughter who marries for love not property or money. She ponders the different fates of Jane Fairfax and Mrs Churchill. "The contrast between Mrs Churchill's importance in the world, and Jane Fairfax's, struck her; one was everything, the other nothing, and she sat musing on the difference of woman's destiny..." (44).

But though capable of thinking like this, Emma herself, as we know, is hypersensitively aware of her social position. Take her reaction to Harriet turning out to be the "daughter of a tradesman – quite respectable":

> *Such was the blood of gentility which Emma had formerly been ready to vouch for! – It was likely to be as untainted, perhaps, as the blood of many a gentleman: but what a connection had she been preparing for Mr Knightley – or for the Churchills – or even for Mr Elton! – The stain of illegitimacy, unbleached by nobility or wealth, would have been a stain indeed. (55)*

This is a brilliant and subtle example of free indirect speech: here, in what Tony Tanner calls Emma's "unconsidered reflex", we see her society thinking *through* her, as it were. The use of the word "perhaps" is, says Tanner,

> a wonderfully revealing hesitation and qualification perfectly placed after the initial speculation which briefly suspends the socially imposed notions of what may or may not be "untainted blood" – "as untainted as the blood

of many a gentleman".

With her horror at the idea of a stained or "unbleached" connection, Emma, in Tanner's view, is "mindlessly internalising or reiterating the crass inequalities of her society". What kind of society is it that regards rank and money as sufficient "bleach" for an unlucky draw in the lottery of life? The answer, of course, is "all too many" societies. The word "bleach", too, is brilliantly chosen: by using it Austen reduces rank and money to the equivalent of a common household product, thus

HOW *EMMA* WAS RECEIVED

As Claire Tomalin notes in her biography, Jane Austen was far from confident how *Emma* would go down. "My greatest anxiety at present," she wrote to a friend, "is that this 4th work shd not disgrace what was good in the others... I am very strongly haunted by the idea that to those readers who have preferred P&P it will appear inferior in Wit, & to those who have preferred MP, very inferior in good sense." Early responses were not reassuring. Among her large family, two of her brothers, Francis and Charles, liked it best of her works so far – Charles read it three times in quick succession – but the rest preferred *Pride and Prejudice* and *Mansfield Park*. The great Mr Jeffrey of the Edinburgh Review was "kept up by it three nights", yet nothing appeared in the Edinburgh.

Austen's publisher, John Murray, had reservations of his own. He sent a copy to Walter Scott, suggesting he devastatingly compounding the irony.

Social life in Highbury does not belong to a pastoral idyll either. Box Hill is a failure, Donwell marred by the presence of Mrs Elton, and the Coles's party distinguished, we are told, by the usual rate of conversation; a few clever things were said, a few downright silly, but by much the larger proportion neither the one nor the other – nothing worse than everyday remarks, dull repetitions, old news, and heavy jokes.

Social occasions in *Emma*, as Ian Watt points out, tend to be marked by hostility and constraint,

should write something about it in the Quarterly Review, but introducing it disloyally with the remark: "Have you any fancy to dash off an article on *Emma*? It wants incidence and romance does it not?" Scott did dash off an article, praising Austen faintly for "copying from nature as she really exists in the common walks of life" and more warmly for her "quiet yet comic dialogue, in which the characters of the speakers evolve themselves with dramatic effect". But his review was half-hearted, and he found both Mr Woodhouse and Miss Bates tiresome. Ten years after Austen's death, however, he was much more fulsome.

That young lady has a talent for describing the involvements and feelings and characters of ordinary life, which is to me the most wonderful I have ever met with. The Big Bow-Wow strain I can do myself like any now going; but the exquisite touch which renders ordinary common-place things and characters interesting from the truth of the description and the sentiment is denied to me. ∎

with the Westons' party at the beginning setting the tone and serving "as a symbolic prelude". Isabella Knightley patronises Mrs Churchill – "What a blessing she never had any children! Poor little creatures, how unhappy she would have made them!"(14) – while her husband, John Knightley, torments Mr Woodhouse by teasing him mercilessly about the snow.

> *"This will prove a spirited beginning to your winter engagements, sir. Something new for your coachman and horses to be making their way through a storm of snow." (15)*

When others try to comfort the old man, John Knightley, "pursuing his triumph rather unfeelingly", continues sardonically:

> *"I admired your resolution very much, sir... in venturing out in such weather... Another hour or two's snow can hardly make the road impassable; and we are two carriages; if one is blown over in the bleak part of the common field there will be the other at hand..."*

John Knightley's "gleeful malice" towards poor Mr Woodhouse's timidity, as Watt points out, can

Mr Knightley tosses his nephews up to the ceiling. "It is such enjoyment to them, that if their uncle did not lay down the rule of their taking turns, whichever began would never give way to the other," says Emma.

be partly excused by his "ideology; he is unkind only in pursuit of a higher truth". That truth is the pointless folly of social life in general, and of dinner parties in particular which, in John Knightley's view, are "in defiance of the laws of nature". It is a truth which the novel partly reflects, one of its major themes, as Janet Todd notes, being "life's tedium and how to make it bearable".

For Emma, Mr Knightley is what will make it bearable. In a sense, she is right when she boasts to Harriet in Chapter Ten that she has no need to get married; unlike most of Austen's heroines, she has no financial reason to give up being single.

> *"I know myself, Harriet, mine is an active, busy mind; with a great many independent resources; and I do not perceive why I should be more in want of employment at forty or fifty than one-and-twenty." (10)*

This is a typically profound misreading of herself and of the human condition. She will come to know herself better by the end of the novel, when she – and we – are reminded how different her fate might be. Realising both that she loves Mr Knightley and that, thanks to her own errors, she may lose him, she is suddenly haunted by the possibility of ending up lonely and miserable with the people she knows dispersing for one marital reason or another:

Hartfield must be comparatively deserted; and she left to cheer her father with the spirits only of ruined happiness... All that were good would be withdrawn... what would remain of cheerful or of rational society within their reach? (48)

For all John Knightley's acid remarks about social life and dinner parties, the real "evil" or terror in Emma's situation is the prospect of having no one to talk to, no real community to be part of, only long evenings with her father to be got through with the aid of games of backgammon. For a person with Emma's "wonderful velocity of thought", this would be almost intolerable.

Instead she ends the novel happy and settled in a relationship of what has been described as "intelligent love". And, one might argue, she deserves it. She endures all kinds of setbacks and vexing developments without self-pity and without showing any impatience. Unlike Mrs Elton, she understands the constraints of society and the importance of public opinion. As Claudia Johnson writes, what makes Mrs Elton so intolerable is not that she is new money and Emma old, or even that Mrs Elton pretends to prerogatives of status Emma has come by honestly. No: Mrs Elton's "exertions of leadership set our teeth on edge because of their insistent publicity..." Emma may feel condescending, but never shows it. Mrs Elton shows it constantly, bullying Jane, colluding with her husband at the ball to humiliate Harriet for her upstart pretensions, loudly telling everyone that she has chosen a special dress for the Westons' party, "in compliment to [them] – who I have no doubt are giving this party chiefly to do me honour..." At her worst, when she transgresses at Box Hill or discloses her suspicions of Jane to Frank Churchill, Emma behaves as badly. But shameful as Emma's infractions are, says Johnson, "they stand out precisely because they are so infrequent, and if Mrs Elton's presence on the scene helps us to identify and to deplore them, it also helps us appreciate how much better Emma handles herself by comparison".

Unlike Mrs Elton, Emma knows the importance of other people's good opinion and, with very rare exceptions, restrains any impulse to abuse, even tolerating Mrs Elton's presumption without sarcasms or protest. And while Mrs Elton boasts of her cara sposo, Emma goes on quietly calling the man she marries Mr Knightley.

The difference between Mrs Elton and Emma is a reminder that a novel which often seems to value openness and directness also values reticence. As Fiona Stafford notes in her introduction to the 1996 Penguin edition, "the possibility of revealing too much is constantly suggested", and the text is full of episodes in which the characters blush, colour, glow or turn red from embarrassment when they say too much, or almost say too much. (*Emma* has more blushes in it than any other Austen novel, notes John Mullan.) Life is perplexing: some of the things that happen around us cannot be understood, however hard we try: the engagement between Frank and Jane depends on secrecy, for example, and, perhaps, embodies that intuition of reality summed up by W.H. Auden: "We are lived by powers we pretend to understand:/They arrange our loves."

Even *Emma* itself often leaves us guessing. We never know what is in Robert Martin's letter, or what the mystery third word is in the alphabet game, or the extent to which Mr Knightley engineers Martin's reconciliation with Harriet, or the exact nature of the "misunderstandings" between Jane and Frank, or, as we have seen, the words with which Emma accepts Mr Knightley. And while there is a perpetual undercurrent of sexual excitement in the novel, says Fiona Stafford, it rarely surfaces (see p.122).

Full knowledge of what goes on around us is neither possible nor desirable, *Emma* suggests, and while its heroine knows herself better than she once did by the time she marries, she by no means knows herself perfectly. Misunderstanding and thus miscommunication are part of our world, and can't be escaped. "The illusion of perfect and total clarity is as much of a fiction as 'the perfect happiness of the union' which concludes the book," says Tony Tanner.

Yet, as John Bayley puts it, harmony, even intimacy, "can exist in a community without mutual understanding – indeed must do, for we must live as we can". This acceptance of misunderstanding is surely the "keynote" of the novel: "Emma is Emma still, as Lydia – at the end of *Pride and Prejudice* – is Lydia still." Most things, Austen reminds us, "must ever be unintelligible to her", as most things are unintelligible to us all. Even the best minds are fallible and limited; our judgements are always subjective and often, in one way or another, prejudiced.

Bayley thinks Austen's final two novels – *Emma* and *Persuasion* – have a comparable effect:

> It seems to me that the harmony established in both between a deep and serious acknowledgement of the unrecorded, unremitted sadness of things, and the never quite impossible *peripeteia* of joy and surprise, gives them a unique status as fictional masterpieces.

The ending of *Emma* is a happy one but the world Emma lives in – small, limited, provincial – is one in which life, for much of the time, is tedious and unrewarding, filled with meaningless social engagements and the need to be polite to bores like Miss Bates or ridiculous figures like Mrs Elton. Austen's view of society and of social occasions is less reassuring in *Emma* than in her early novels: after one evening in Hartfield we read that "every thing was relapsing into its usual state. Former provocations reappeared. The aunt was as tiresome as ever..." (20). People scatter. Jane, the friend Emma should have had, will leave, having married, with Frank; Emma will be left with Mr Knightley – and her father.

The novel's world is one distinguished by a troubling mixture of openness, so far as words will permit openness, and concealment; a world in which unhappiness is more common than happiness, but in which happiness is possible – possible but elusive, depending a great deal on luck and temperament and easily thrown away through egoism, vanity and a lack of self-knowledge. And rarely is the happiness perfect. "Perfect happiness, even in memory, is not common" (27), reflects Emma in one of the quasi-Johnsonian aphorisms which sometimes slide into her interior monologues.

What had she to wish for? Nothing, but to grow more worthy of him, whose intentions and judgement had been ever so superior to her own. Nothing, but that the lessons of her past folly might teach her humility and circumspection in future. (54)

This is Emma towards the end, thinking vivaciously, extravagantly, hopefully – as usual.

READING IN *EMMA*

Reading, as the acceptable pastime of the educated lady or gentleman, had come under intense scrutiny since before Austen's time. While foreigners were impressed "by the passion for reading and education shown by a wide cross-section of the English", according to Roy Porter (*English Society in the Eighteenth Century*), certain books, and particularly the emerging genre of the novel, were often attacked as corruptive to the intellect. "Where the reading of novels prevails as a habit," wrote Coleridge, "it occasions in time the entire destruction of the powers of the mind." Austen's own view is perhaps most eloquently expressed in *Northanger Abbey,* published posthumously in 1818:

> I will not adopt that ungenerous and impolitic custom so common with novel-writers, of degrading by their contemptuous censure the very performances, to the number of which they are themselves adding – joining with their greatest enemies in bestowing the harshest epithets on such works, and scarcely ever permitting them to be read by their own heroine, who, if she accidentally take up a novel, is sure to turn over its insipid pages with disgust. (5)

Strikingly, the voiceless Mr Martin is the only character in *Emma* whose reading habits are discussed in full, when the heroine questions Harriet as to the young man's tastes and intentions. We learn that "he reads the Agricultural Reports, and some other books that lay in one of the window seats... but he reads *them* all to himself" (4). The next sentence indicates a delineation between business and pleasure for the gentleman farmer, since during Harriet's visits "he would read something aloud out of The Elegant Extracts; very entertaining. And I know he has read *The Vicar of Wakefield*." He has also "never read... *The Romance of the Forest*, nor *The Children of the Abbey*. He had never heard of such books before I mentioned them; but now, he is determined to get them as soon as ever he can."

The last three were all popular novels of the time. *The Vicar of Wakefield,* a comic melodrama by Oliver Goldsmith, was first published in 1766; *The Romance of the Forest,* by Ann Radcliffe (1791), and *The Children of the Abbey,* by Regina Maria Roche (1798), are both gothic tales. Though hardly the most extensive reading list, the passage illustrates several of Mr Martin's best qualities; his basic good sense, hard-working temperament, and awareness of others' sensibilities. The eagerness to follow up Harriet's very prosaic recommendations is a similar romantic gesture to the walnuts and the serenading by his shepherd's boy.

For the rest of Highbury, literary influence is conveyed in conversation, by references, quotation *and* misquotation – suitably enough for a novel so concerned with the difficulties inherent in communication.

Sometimes what the speakers intend to express runs entirely against the meaning of the quoted text. Mr Woodhouse links a bawdy verse by David Garrick – "Kitty, a fair but frozen maid", about a lady with a very questionable history – to his beloved, decidedly genteel Isabella. The riddle is full of sexual innuendo and suggests many different interpretations before its final solution – chimney sweep; a slang term for sexual intercourse – is fixed on by the end. Characteristically, Mr Woodhouse fails to grasp any of this.

There is a similarly humorous tone to many of Mrs Elton's declamations, made still more potent by their speaker's vain pretensions. In Chapter 52 she inadvertently likens Mr Frank Churchill to the bull in "The Hare and Many Friends" by John Gay:

> Love calls me hence; a fav'rite cow
> Expects me near yon barley's mow
> For when a lady's in the case
> You know all other things give place.

As with Mr Woodhouse, the inappropriate nature of the remark escapes Mrs Elton entirely. Meanwhile, her reference to "Hymen's saffron robe" (John Milton, *L'Allegro*) and her reflections on how, with regard to Jane Fairfax, "full many a flower is born to blush unseen/And waste its fragrance on the desert air" (Gray's *Elegy Written in a Country Churchyard*), are pure affectation. Ronald Blythe's commentary on 'The literary tastes of Highbury' (*Emma*, 1966 edition) notes that Mrs Elton is a "gifted debaser of art who reduces each quotation to a sentimental